DON'T JUST SURF

effective research strategies
for the Net

SECOND EDITION

Maureen Henninger

UNSW PRESS

Thanks must go to my family, friends and colleagues who have encouraged me in this effort.

Most of all I would like to thank my colleague, Visiting Professor Carmel Maguire, who not only suggested this book, but patiently read the manuscript and offered invaluable suggestions.

A UNSW PRESS BOOK

Published by
UNIVERSITY OF NEW SOUTH WALES PRESS
University of New South Wales
Sydney 2052 Australia

© Maureen Henninger 1999

First published 1997
First reprint 1997
Second reprint 1998
Second edition 1999

National Library of Australia
Cataloguing-in Publication entry:

Henninger, Maureen, 1940- .
Don't Just Surf: effective research strategies for the Net

2nd ed.
Bibliography.
Includes index.
ISBN 0 86840 656 2.

1. Internet (Computer network). 2. Research — Methodology.
3. Research — Computer network resources. I. Title.

001.402854678

Printed by BPA, Victoria

Contents

Preface

In the preface of the first edition I wrote 'the phenomenon of the Internet is being talked about by nearly everyone...anyone who has even superficially 'surfed' the Internet will know that there is a great deal of 'information' out there! A huge amount of it is rubbish (bearing in mind that one person's trash is another's treasure), but finding what you want among the millions of documents is not easy. At the time I wrote this, there were estimated to be about 16 million Internet 'host domains', that is, computers holding publicly available information. By July 1998 the *Internet Domain Survey* counted over 36 million host domains, and there are estimates of over 300 million documents!

The difficulties of finding authoritative information to satisfy your requirements are growing as fast as the Internet itself. It seems there are new search tools every week and the 'old', familiar ones are constantly evolving. Effective Internet searching in this ever-expanding environment requires new strategies. This second edition examines new Web developments, looks at the latest trends in search tools and provides strategies for using them.

I would like to thank everyone who has provided me with valuable feedback from the first edition. I have incorporated many of your suggestions in this new edition and many of you will note the new section, *People are information resources* — a fact that we all recognise and need to exploit. And again I would like to express my appreciation to all those individuals who freely contribute to the wealth of research material on the Internet itself.

Maureen Henninger

1 The Internet

Overview

The Internet is a global network of computer networks. At first it was confined to those networks using the Internet protocols (*IP protocol*, a set of rules for computers to communicate) which allow their collective users access to the publicly available files on all of them.

IP networks include:

1. National networks:
   - some publicly supported, for example *EdNA* (Education Network Australia);
   - some commercial, such as Telstra's *On Australia*;
   - some not-for-profit, for example *AARNet* (Australian Academic and Research Network).
2. Regional networks such as New York State Education and Research Network (*NYSERnet*), and *VICnet* Victoria's Network.
3. Campus-wide networks, for example the UNSW Campus Wide Network; this category is often referred to as a **CWIS** (a campus-wide information service).

The Internet had its beginnings in 1969 with the establishment of *ARPANet* (Advanced Research Projects Network) of the US Defence Department.   In the 1980s the National Science Foundation established a network (*NSFnet*) which was designed to provide access to several supercomputer centres for its grant recipients.   In 1988 this displaced the *ARPANet* as the national wide-area network in the US.

Soon it spread to some non-IP-based networks (for example, *BITnet*, *DECnet*) which made connections called *gateways*, intended at first just to transfer electronic mail between the Internet and their own network. Most of these gateways have grown into full service translators between the networks, and for all intents and purposes these non-IP networks are also part of the Internet. Since then the Internet has expanded throughout the world. Carvin (1996) is a very good source on the Internet for a brief history.

Who owns the Internet?

The Internet is decentralised which means each network is managed locally. The Internet network itself is owned by no-one, but used by all. It is governed, however, by the Internet Society (ISOC), a voluntary, international collective of researchers, academics and users who determine the future of the network.

2 The World Wide Web

Overview

The World Wide Web, otherwise known as the Web, was developed in 1989 by at team led by Tim Berner-Lee at CERN (Conseil Européen pour la Recherché Nucleaire), the European Laboratory for Particle Physics in Geneva, Switzerland. This development led to the enormous popularity of the Internet. The Web is based on a technology called *hypertext* which allows textual information to be organised in a non-linear fashion using links within documents and between documents.

Hypertext is a term first used by an American, Ted Nelson, in 1960 to describe his Xanadu project, a publishing system 'intended to store a body of writings as an interconnected whole, with linkages, and to provide instantaneous access to any writings within that body' (Nelson, 1980). He defined hypertext as 'a body of written or pictorial material interconnected in such a complex way that it could not be conveniently represented on paper. It may contain summaries or maps of its contents and their interrelations; it may contain annotations, additions and footnotes from scholars who have examined it' (Nelson, 1965). Nelson also coined the term 'hypermedia' which means hypertext with multimedia; for example, a document that includes graphics, photographs, video clips and sound.

The Web attempts to organise all information on the Internet as a set of hypertext and hypermedia documents, some of which may in turn have hypertext links to other documents. Web documents are often referred to as Web 'pages'.

Browsers

The Web is accessed by using a *browser*, a piece of software which you need to install on your computer and which enables you to look at information stored on the Web. The most sophisticated browsers can display hypermedia files; these may be text, hypertext, graphics, sound, video or animations. Less sophisticated browsers such as *Lynx* can display only text. The most popular browsers are *Netscape*, *Explorer*, and *Mosaic*. The browser locates the initial site/computer (the URL, Uniform Resource Locator) to retrieve a 'document', interprets the document formatting (HTML, Hypertext Markup Language) and presents, that is, displays the 'document' to the user with as much embellishment as the browser is capable of providing.

You move around the Web by pointing with the mouse and clicking, that is, by depressing the mouse button on any hypertext link. These hypertext links are items, sometimes text and sometimes icons (small pictures) which are highlighted, for example in **blue,** or **underlined** (or both).

Figures 2.1–2.3 show Web documents displayed by the most popular browsers, *Netscape Communicator* **4.0**, *Netscape* **3.0**, and Microsoft's *Internet Explorer.*

The examples in this book use *Netscape Communicator Version 4.0* for *Windows.* Figure 2.1 shows the various parts of the screen (the interface) — the interfaces of other browsers are similar. Chapter 3 gives a detailed tutorial on how to use *Netscape Communicator.*

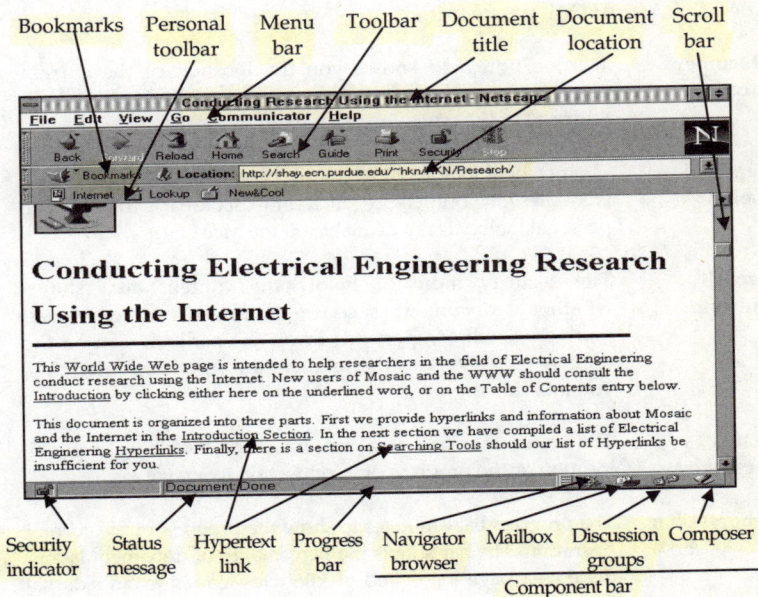

Figure 2.1 A document on the World Wide Web (*Netscape Communicator* 4.0)

Below is an explanation of these items on the screen:

Menu bar   When you click on an item on the menu bar, a pull-down menu of options is displayed.

Toolbar   Toolbar buttons activate the Netscape features you'll most commonly use. **Note**: in *Netscape* 4 the *Search* and *Guide* buttons take you to search engines and guide chosen by *Netscape*.

Document title   The title of the document as specified by the author in the HTML source text.

Document location   The location field shows you the location of the current page and can be used to enter the location (the URL address) of the page you wish to go to next.

Personal toolbar   The personal toolbar allows you to create buttons that link to web sites of your choice, including bookmark folders. The personal toolbar is not available on the Mac OS).

Security indicator   The security indicator below the content area shows whether a document is secure or insecure (open/closed padlock) — clicking on this or on the padlock icon on the toolbar will give you the security information of the page you are viewing.

Status message   The status message area contains text describing a page's location or the progress of a connection to a page.

Progress bar   The progress bar animates to show the progress of the current operation. The bar shows the percentages of document layout done as a page loads and of kilobytes loaded as an external image loads.

Component bar   *Netscape* 4 has a component bar which allows you to move from one application to another — *Browser, Mailbox, Discussion* and *Composer*.

Scroll bar   The scroll bar moves you vertically through the document with the aid of a mouse.

Figure 2.2 Document on *Netscape 3.0* browser

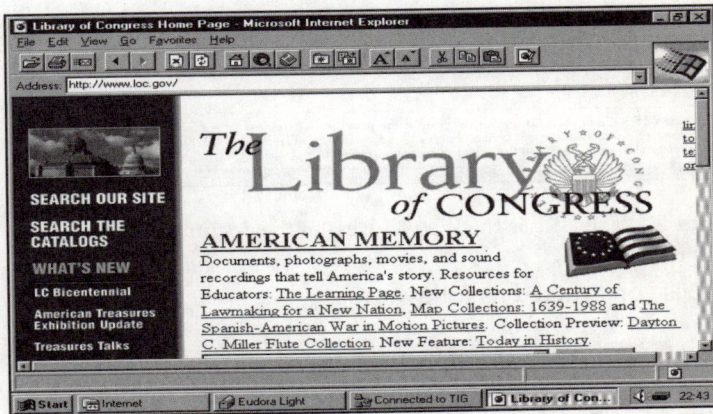

Figure 2.3 Document on *Internet Explorer* browser

Uniform Resource Locators (URLs)

A Uniform Resource Locator (referred to as a URL) is the Web address of a document. It is the unique address of a single HTML page or file on the Web. The browser shows the URL in a field labelled **Location** or **Netsite**.

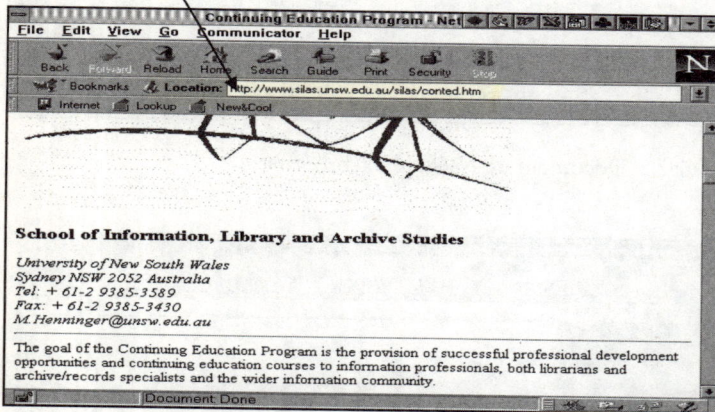

Figure 2.4 The URL is the Web address of the document

A URL is constructed as follows:

source type://host domain/path or directory/filename

http://www.silas.unsw.edu.au/silas/conted.htm

The *source type* specifies which protocol should be used to retrieve the 'document', which in most cases is a hypertext document and so the **http** (Hypertext Transfer Protocol) source type is used. The *host domain* is the name of the computer on which the 'document' is stored. In the case of a hypertext document, the filename has the extension **html** or **htm** (Hypertext Markup Language).

However, there are other source types which are services or processes. Table 2.1 shows the most common ones.

Table 2.1 Examples of URLs

Source type	Protocol or service	Example URL
Web document	http://	http://www.silas.unsw.edu.au/conted.htm
Gopher	gopher://	gopher://gopher.info.anu.edu.au
File transfer protocol	ftp://	ftp://ftp.mel.dit.csiro.au
Telnet (remote login)	telnet://	telnet://library.unsw.edu.au
Email	mailto:	mailto:m.henninger@unsw.edu.au
Network news	news:	news:bit.listserv.allmusic
Local file	file:///	file:///c|/local.htm

Accessing URLs

Web documents or pages can be accessed by several different methods. *Netscape Navigator* has three methods.

Method 1

1. Select **File** from the menu bar, then **Open Page**.

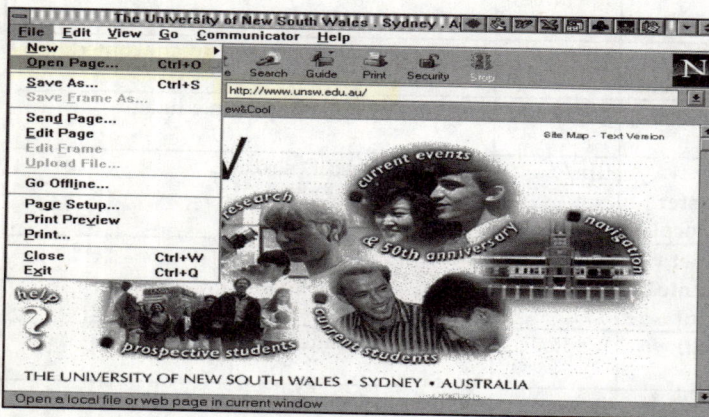

Figure 2.5 Opening a URL from the main *Netscape* menu

2. Type in the URL in the template presented and click on **Open**.

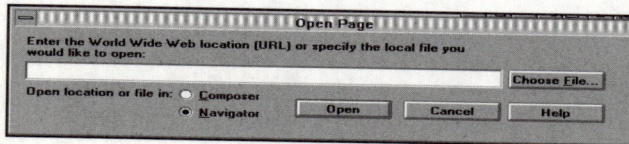

Figure 2.6 Template for opening a URL

Method 2

Place the cursor in the **Go to** bar and type in the URL.

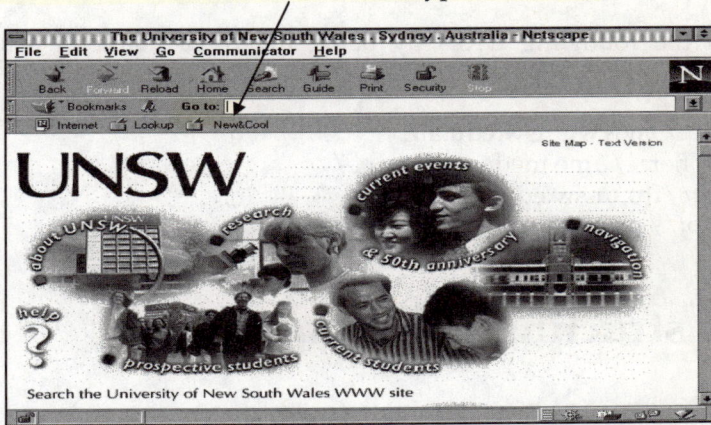

Figure 2.7 Opening a URL by typing directly into the **Go to** bar

If you are using *Netscape* **3.0** or **4.0** you can omit the prefix **http://** — it is automatically added.

Method 3

Select and access the URLs from your **navigation history list** or **bookmarks** (see the *Navigation history* and *Bookmarks* sections in Chapter 3).

Accessing URLs exercises

Open the following URLs by using the three methods listed above:

1. http://www.unsw.edu.au
2. gopher://ume.med.ucalgary.ca/
3. ftp://ftp.unsw.edu.au/
4. http://sunsite.berkeley.edu/InternetIndex/

Constructing home page URLs

A *home page* is the public face of an organisation or a person on the Web. Generally its URL consists of the name of the web server (the host computer) and its *domain name* which locates the organisation on the Internet. If you are looking for information specific to one organisation, it is often quicker to go straight to its home page rather than relying on some of the Internet search tools.

To be able to construct a home page URL, you need to understand the Internet's Domain Name System (DNS).

The Domain Name System

The Domain Name System (DNS) is the method used for naming and locating computers on the Internet. The *IP address* (*Internet Protocol*) of a computer is a number, for example **149.171.53.52**. These numbers are hard to remember, therefore we use a domain name which is more easily remembered. The DNS locates the domain name and then translates it into the IP address. Because it would be very difficult to maintain one central database or list of IP addresses and domain names, these lists are distributed throughout the Internet in a hierarchy of authority.

In other words the DNS consists of:

- the country (international authority);
- the type of organisation (national Internet Society authority);
- the name of the organisation (national authority);
- the name of the department (organisational authority);
- the name of the computer (departmental authority).

Each of these is separated by a dot, '.', with no spaces.

For example, in **www.silas.unsw.edu.au**

www	is the name of the computer in the department (Web server, a computer which stores Web documents)
silas	is the name of the department (School of Information, Library & Archive Studies)
unsw	is the name of the organisation (University of New South Wales)
edu	is the type of organisation (educational)
au	is the country code (Australia).

A URL is read from right to left, as postal employees read addresses on envelopes from bottom to top. Thus the top level domains in a URL are the country codes and the organisational types. The country code is an international standard allocated by the International Organization for Standardization (ISO). On the other hand, the domain name for the type of an organisation is a national standard and differs slightly from country to country; Australia has adopted the US standard, but other countries, for example UK and New Zealand, use variations. Table 2.2 lists a selection of ISO country codes and the organisation type domains of the US, New Zealand and the United Kingdom.

Table 2.2 Selected domains (Australia, New Zealand, UK, US)

ISO country codes	Country/Organisation types
au	Australia
ca	Canada
fr	France
nz	New Zealand
us	United States (generally left off)
Major organisation types *Australia and US*	
com	commercial
edu	educational
gov	government
mil	military
net	network
org	non-government organisation
New Zealand varieties	
ac	tertiary educational institutions
co	commercial
cri	Crown Research Institutes
gen	individuals and general purposes
govt	government
iwi	Maori organisations
school	primary & secondary schools
UK varieties	
ac	academic
co	commercial
gov	government, except Defence (**mod**)
ltd	limited companies
plc	publicly listed companies
sch	schools

For a full listing of country codes see:
http://www.cs.mu.oz.au/~langs/countries.html

Increasing standardisation continues to make the construction of previously unknown URLs more intuitive. Following are some of these developments:

- The de facto standard for naming a web server is **www.**
- Most organisations, if their name is a single word, register it as their domain (*Netscape*, Sun) or as an acronym, if the name has several words (for example UNSW for the University of New South Wales, BBC for the British Broadcasting Corporation).

Coopers, a brewery in Australia	http://www.coopers.com.au
Australian Broadcasting Corporation	http://www.abc.net.au
EC Consultants, England	http://www.ecc.co.uk/
New Zealand Government	http://www.govt.nz

- Government and university departments are often included in abbreviated form before the organisation's name.

New South Wales Government	http://www.nsw.gov.au
New South Wales Health Department	http://www.health.nsw.gov.au

Browser 'intuition'

The newest versions of the *Netscape* and *Explorer* browsers have added facilities to make it easier to find an organisation's URL.

If the URL is in the US, is a Web site and is in the **.com** domain, you need only to type the organisation domain. For example, for http://www.hotbot.com you simply type **hotbot**.

If the the organisation is not American or not commercial, simply type a '**?**' in the location bar, along with whatever information you have. This will invoke the *Excite* search engine that searches titles and URLs for a match. This may be helpful.

For Australian URLs Charles Sturt University maintains a register of Australian Web servers <http://www.csu.edu.au/links/ozweb.html>.

URL construction exercises

Try constructing the URLs for the home pages of the following organisations:

1. The Australian company *Sausage*.
2. The Government of the Northern Territory (Australia).
3. The National Library of Australia.
4. The New Zealand Customs (government entity).
5. Harvard University in the United States.
6. The Australian Archives.
7. The NSW Department of Health.
8. Cambridge University, UK (*note:* Oxford and Cambridge are abbreviated to **ox** and **cam**).
9. Curtis Davis Garrard, a law firm in London.
10. The Smithsonian Institution, an educational organisation in the United States.

You will probably have no trouble with at least 50 per cent of these exercises, and you may be convinced that it is worthwhile trying to construct the URL for the home page of an organisation rather than searching for it on the Internet.

3 Using *Netscape*

The following section is a brief tutorial on some of the useful features of *Netscape* Navigator 4.0 for *Windows*.

Navigation history

Each time a hypertext link is activated, the requested document is retrieved and displayed. Once a 'document' is displayed on the screen, it is placed in *cache* (the system holds it temporarily in cache memory), so the browser does not need to retrieve it again from the remote site. This 'cached' file is an ASCII file with the embedded HTML tags.

Netscape **4.0** keeps two history lists of the web sites you have visited. One is found under the **Go** menu item and is the same as *Netscape* **3.0**'s history list which holds up to 10 items during the **current** session. The second, permanent list holds all visited sites and you can set the number of days they are retained as follows:

1. Select **Edit**, then **Preferences.**
2. Click on **Navigator.**
3. Type in the number of days you wish the sites to remain in your history list.
4. You can also clear the history list from this screen.

Navigator
application

No. of days until
expiration

Clear history list
button

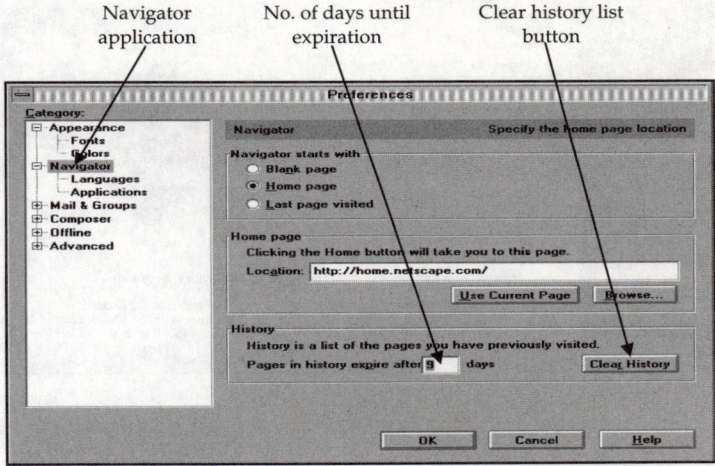

Figure 3.1 Setting the history list in *Netscape* 4.0's **Preferences**

You can revisit these sites by:

- selecting the **Go** button for the history list and clicking on the required site;
- moving sequentially through the previously accessed sites by using the **Back** and **Forward** buttons on the toolbar.

Note that the page currently displayed is marked by a ✓.

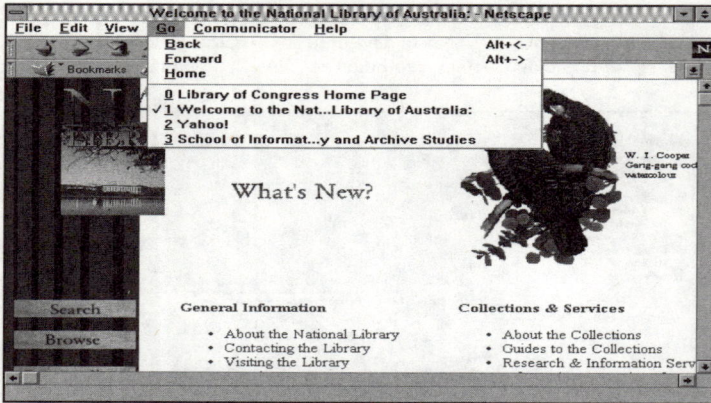

Figure 3.2 Using the *Netscape* **Go** button

To revisit a site by using the history list:

1. Choose **Communicator** from the menu bar.
2. Select **History.**

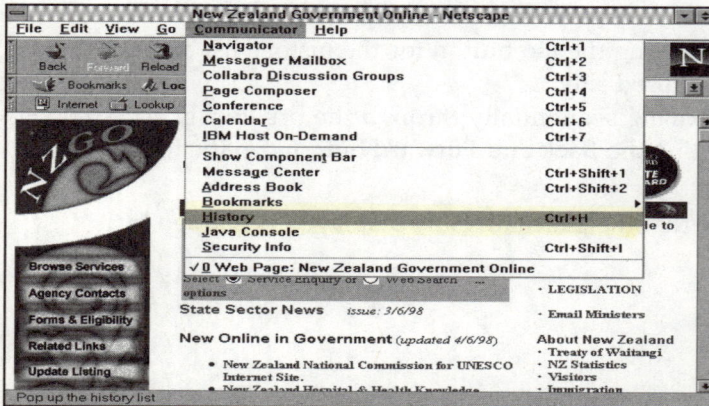

Figure 3.3 Selecting the history list in *Netscape* **4.0**

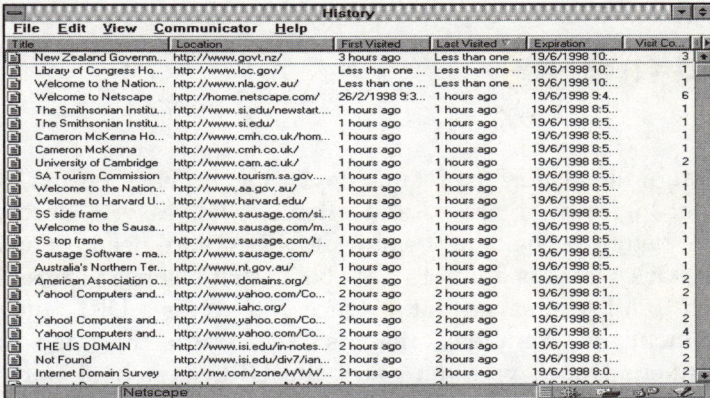

Figure 3.4 The history list in *Netscape* 4.0

Netscape will always retrieve a 'document' from cache if it is there. However, if a Web page has changed since you last visited it, you will have to use the **Reload** button on the toolbar to get the new one. The **Reload** button compares the cache 'document' to the network 'document', and displays the most recent one.

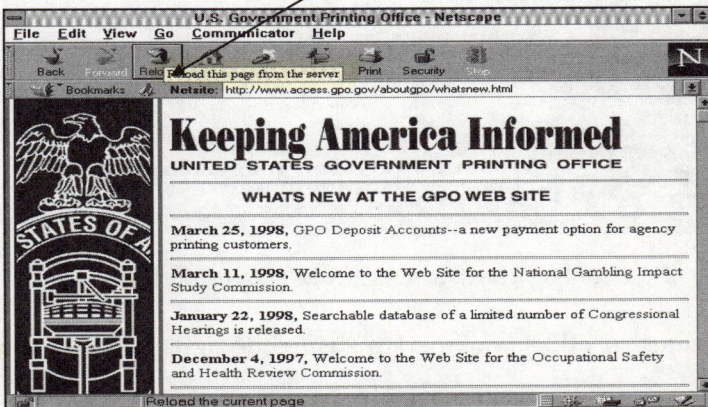

Figure 3.5 *Netscape*'s **Reload** button

Bookmarks

Although the history list retains the URLs you have visited, they are not logically organised and often are not easy to decipher. For a better permanent record of URLs you need to use a **bookmark** which is a link to a Web site that has been saved and added to a list of saved links. Once you access a URL, and the 'document' is complete, that is, the status message says 'Document Done', you can mark the URL as a bookmark by clicking on **Bookmarks** in the toolbar, and selecting the option **Add Bookmark**.

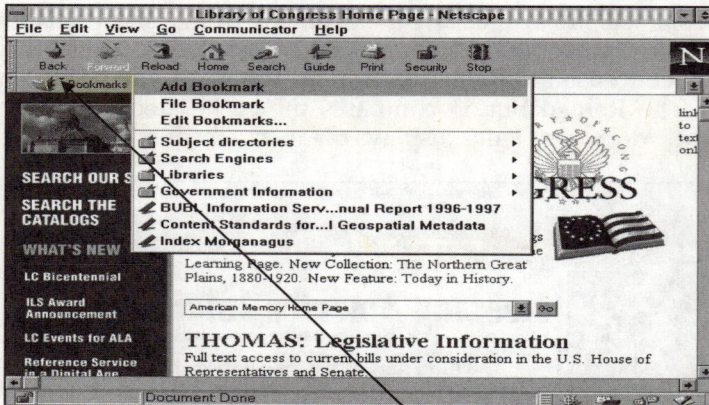

Figure 3.6 Adding a bookmark using the **Bookmarks** tool

You can also add a bookmark by using the right mouse button.

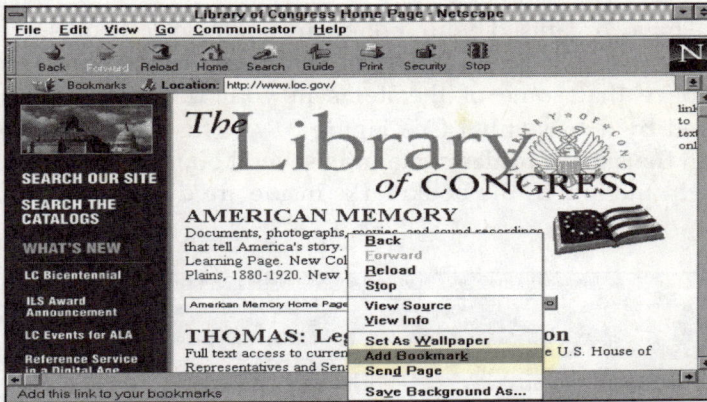

Figure 3.7 Adding a bookmark using the right mouse button

You can then access the bookmarked URL by clicking on it.

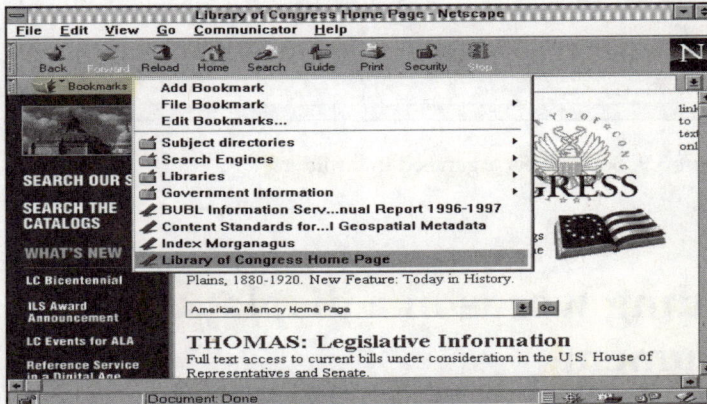

Figure 3.8 Accessing a URL from the **Bookmarks** menu

If you have organised your bookmarks into *folders,* or subject categories (see Chapter 15, '*Organising your information*') you will notice that some of the items in your bookmark list are followed by a ➤ symbol (see Figure 3.9). This means that the item on the list is a **folder** containing several bookmarks. As you highlight the folder, the bookmarks inside are displayed (Figure 3.9).

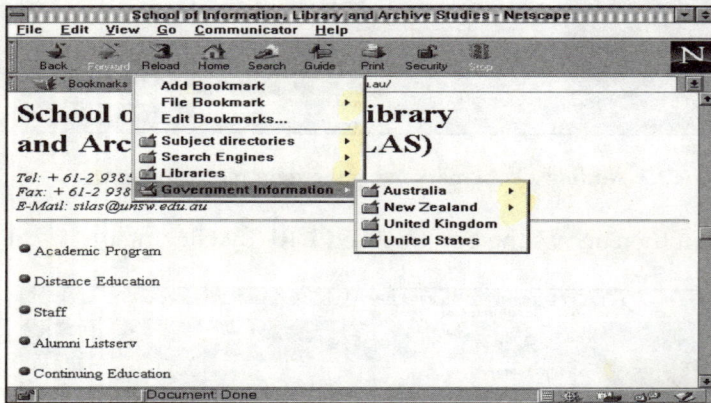

Figure 3.9 Bookmarks organised into folders

Finding words in a displayed document

When a long document has been displayed, you can find a word or phrase within the document by using the **Find in Page** option under **Edit** on the menu bar and typing in the required word or phrase in the window presented. The word or phrase is then found and highlighted in the document.

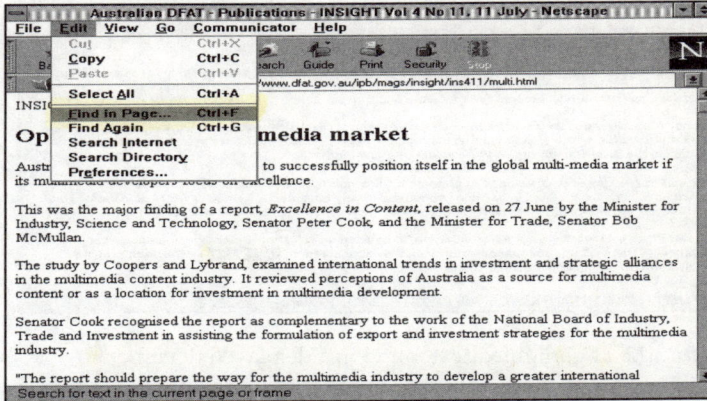

Figure 3.10 **Netscape**'s **Find** option

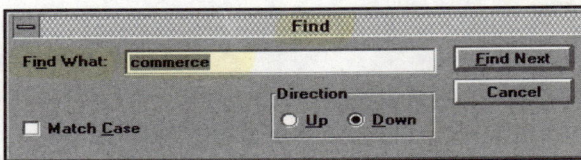

Figure 3.11 Template for finding a word in a document

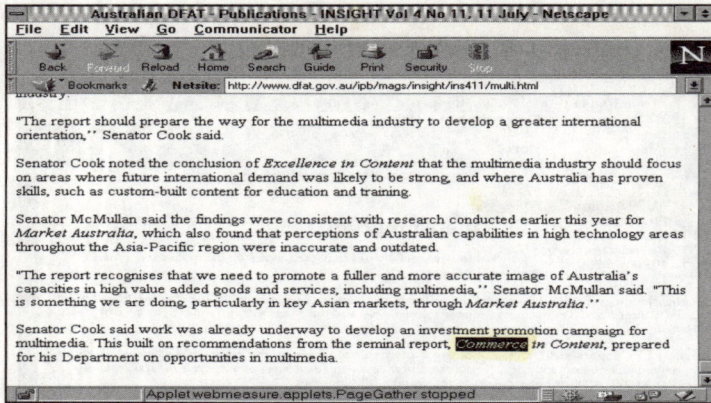

Figure 3.12 Hightlighted text found in a displayed document

Graphics

Downloading or retrieving graphics from the Internet can be very time consuming. Unless the graphic is an integral part of the 'document', you might want to 'turn off' the automatic loading of images simply by clicking on **Automatically load images** option which you will find under the **Advanced Preferences**. The 'non-graphic' mode displays an empty box and any alternative text that may explain what the graphic is (Figure 3.13).

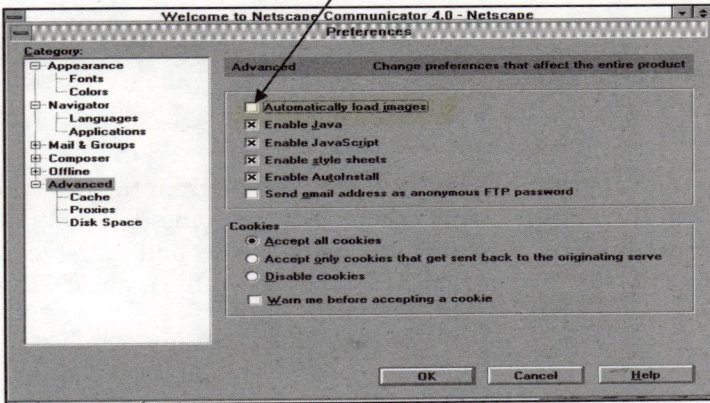

Figure 3.13 Turning off the **Automatically load images** in *Netscape*

You can always look at the images by clicking on the **Images** button on the toolbar.

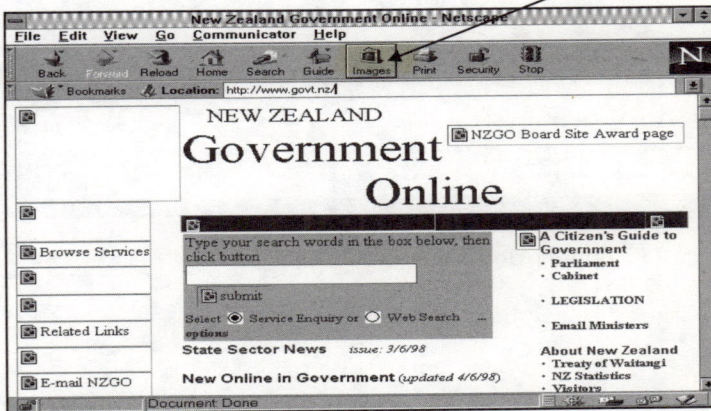

Figure 3.14 *Netscape*'s **Images** button

Printing files

If you wish to print a document, choose **File** from the menu bar and then the option **Print.** There may be some delay because the browser must recontact the remote site and retrieve the document in order to print it, since the cached file is an ASCII file with the HTML tags.

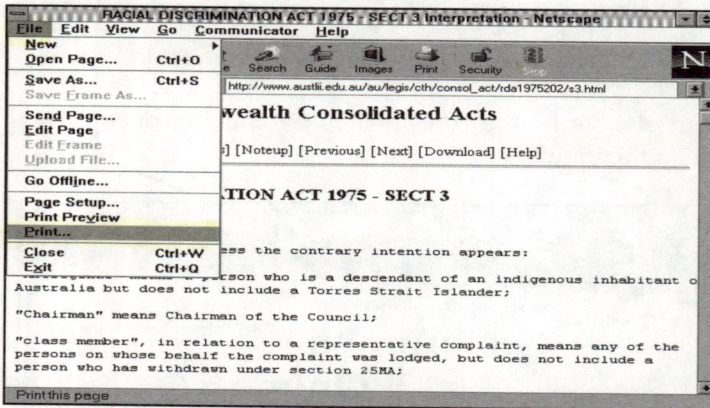

Figure 3.15 Printing documents in *Netscape*

Saving files

If you wish to transfer an item (Web page, downloaded software, etc.) as a file to your computer or to a diskette, use the Internet protocol *FTP* (File Transfer Protocol). *Netscape* does this very simply by **saving** the file.

1. From the menu bar choose **File** and **Save As**.

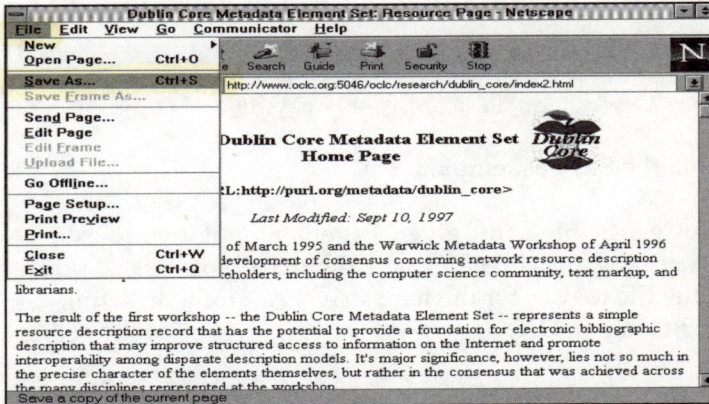

Figure 3.16 Saving documents in *Netscape*

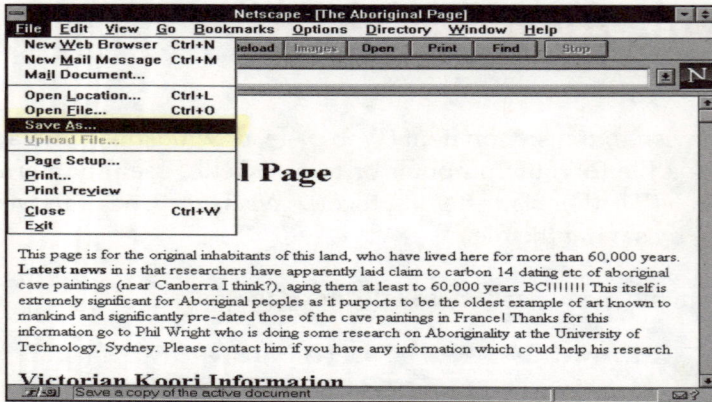

Figure 3.17 Saving a file in **Netscape** *(Windows)*

2. Fill in the **Save as** template by:

   a) using the file name given, or renaming it if you wish;
   b) selecting the directory and the drive you wish to transfer the file to (C:\ for the hard drive, A:\ for a diskette);
   c) clicking on **OK**.

In the example shown in Figure 3.18:

- the filename is **index2.htm**;
- the directory is **a:\internet**; and
- the drive is **a:**.

If the item is a Web document, make sure that it is saved as an HTML file.

Filename   Directory   Drive   OK

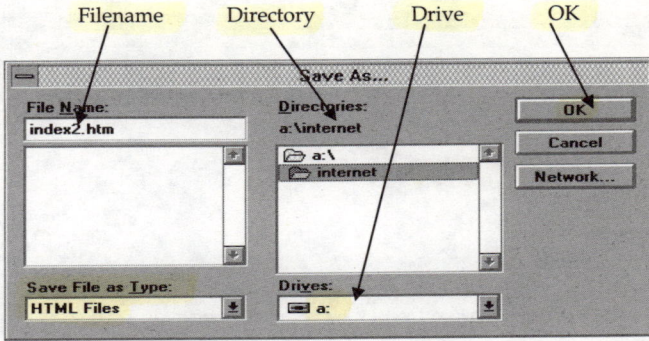

Figure 3.18 **Netscape's Save As** template (*Windows*)

An HTML file contains all the hypertext mark-up language formatting so that as a locally-held file it can be displayed by a browser without opening an Internet connection.

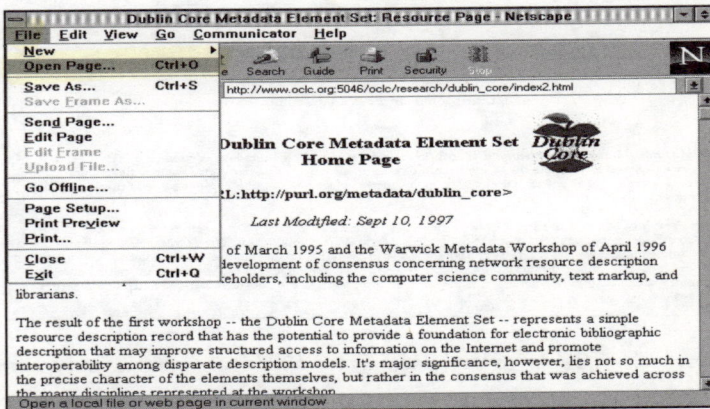

Figure 3.19 **Opening a locally-held file**

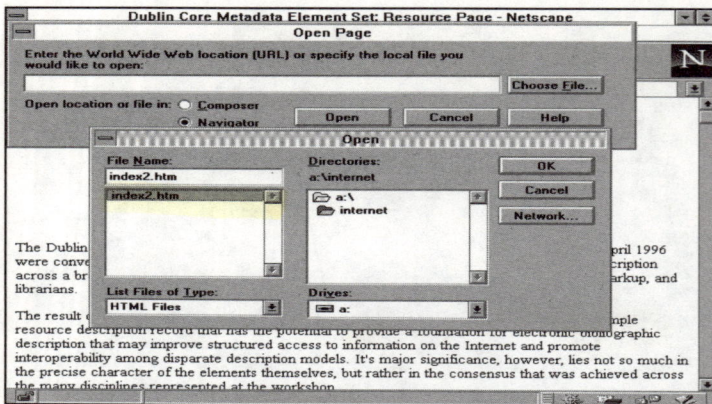

Figure 3.20 Selecting the file to open (*Windows*)

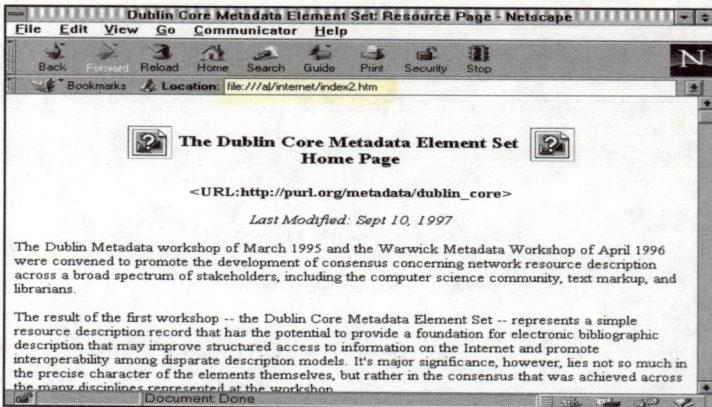

Figure 3.21 A displayed local document — file:///a|/internet/index2.htm

Notice that in Figure 3.21 the graphics are not displayed; in place
of the graphic there is an icon with a '?'. Each graphic in a Web
document is a separate file and therefore has to be saved
individually.

Netscape Help

Netscape provides its **Help Contents** through the **Help** item on the menu bar.

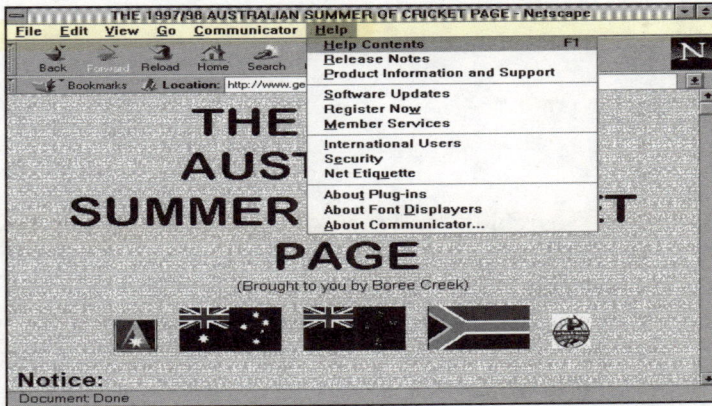

*Figure 3.22 Netscape's **Help** menu*

4 Searching electronic information

Overview

Methods of searching in the digital/online environment, whether the medium is online (a remote database accessed via tele-communications), on a CD-ROM (electronic information stored on a compact disk) or the Internet, depends on the way the documents have been indexed. There are two fundamental methods of indexing:

1. full-text (often referred to as free-text);
2. subject classification.

In Internet terms, these indexes are known as **search engines** (full-text) and **subject guides**, **subject directories or Web directories** (subject classification). For details on these Internet indexes see Chapters 9 and 10.

Full-text indexing/searching

From the point of view of the creator, full-text indexes are advantageous since they are generated by a computer program and therefore are inexpensive to create and maintain. Their size depends on disk space, and theoretically these indexes can provide access to vast numbers of documents or, in the case of the Internet, Web sites. Every word of the document becomes an index term and thus is searchable; this is known as 'keyword' searching. For the searcher, however, there is no indication of synonymous or equivalent relationships between terms: for example between *cats, tigers* or *felines*. Nor are there any contextual relationships (semantic or syntactic associations) embedded in the index: for example 'blind Venetian' is not distinguishable from 'Venetian blind'. The searcher can only rely on the presence (or absence) of the requested word in the document. Searching this type of index can result in a lack of documents because the index terms are too precise, or too many documents, many of which are irrelevant.

Subject classification

Indexes that classify documents into specific subjects (that is, under subject headings) use controlled vocabulary terms. They are expensive to create and maintain since they require intellectual input by a human indexer and this dependence on human time and endeavour constrains the number of documents indexed and the depth of that indexing. However, the context of the index terms is defined, providing semantic associations, and synonymous relationships can be established by the use of a thesaurus, thus overcoming some of the disadvantages of free-text searching. Subject heading searches can provide highly relevant documents, but these searches can also fail to produce any documents if the searcher does not know the contents of the database, or does not know the controlled vocabulary, or if the concept sought is too new to have been assigned a subject heading.

As an example, the following text has been indexed as full-text and has also been classified as a subject heading.

Cats like to catch and eat birds, but also survive on dry or tinned food

Table 4.1 Comparison of full-text and classified indexing

Full-text index	Subject classification
birds catch cats dry eat food like survive tinned	cats — eating habits

Note that although words such as 'to', 'and', 'also', and 'or', indicate semantic relationships, by themselves they have little subject content and are generally not indexed; they are 'stop words'.

If you were looking for information on birds by using a full-text index, you would get this piece of text, which is only peripherally relevant to the subject of 'birds' (unless, of course, you are a bird). On the other hand, if you wanted to know about what cats eat and you did not know that there was a subject heading 'cats — eating habits', you would not retrieve this text. Experienced online searchers know that the systems yielding the most satisfactory results, that is high recall of the most relevant documents, are the ones that use both types of indexing and therefore allow searching by keywords as well as subject headings.

Boolean logic

Many indexes in the online environment provide facilities to refine searches in order to retrieve highly relevant documents. These facilities employ sophisticated search techniques such as:

- *Boolean logic*, a system of logical thought developed by the English mathematician George Boole;
- *proximity operators* which specify the relationship between words (see **'Proximity operators'**, page 41).

Boolean logic is used when the search request contains more than one concept: for example, *legal information in Australia*. There are three Boolean or logical operators — AND, OR and NOT. These operators require the presence or the absence of a term in the document. For a simple search of two terms, the three Boolean operators work as follows:

Table 4.2 Boolean (logical) operators

Operator	Process	Result
OR	Requires either or both terms to be present in the document, for example river **OR** stream.	Increases the number of documents.
AND	Requires both terms to be present, for example river **AND** stream.	Reduces the number of documents.
NOT	Requires the term to be absent, for example river **NOT** stream.	Reduces the number of documents, but runs the risk of eliminating a relevant document.

Boolean logic can be shown diagrammatically. For example:

1. Australia or New Zealand (as shown in Figure 4.1);
2. legal information in Australia (as shown in Figure 4.2);
3. legal information in Australia but not in New Zealand (as shown in Figure 4.3)

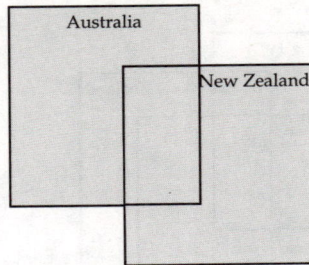

Australia **OR** New Zealand

Figure 4.1 Boolean (logical) operator **OR**

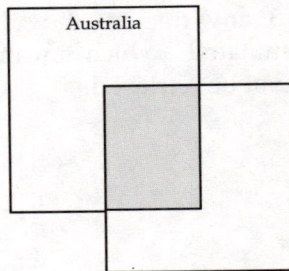

legal information **AND** Australia

Figure 4.2 Boolean (logical) operator **AND**

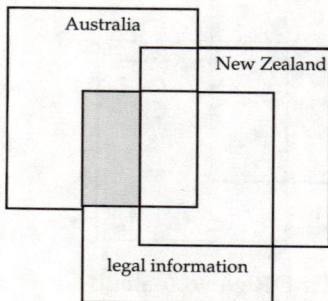

legal information **AND** Australia **NOT** New Zealand

Figure 4.3 Boolean (logical) operators AND, NOT

Note that in Figure 4.3 any document with the term 'New Zealand' has been eliminated, which means that the most relevant document may not be retrieved.

Proximity operators

To establish semantic or contextual relationships between words in full-text searching, proximity operators may be used. They are system-dependent, that is, these operators depend on the parti-cular system being used. What they do is specify where one term in the document must appear in relation to another term — for example, adjacent to, within a certain number of words or in the same sentence or paragraph. Some examples are shown in Table 4.3.

Table 4.3 Proximity operators

Search statement	Result
government **(ADJ)** information	This is a document about **government information**
government **(NEAR)** information	**Information** about the Australian **government**
government **(NEAR 5)** information	A conference on the **government** of New Zealand and its **information** policy

Two other operators often used are SAME and WITH which generally specify that the words must appear in the same sentence or paragraph.

Subject classification and thesauruses

There are many subject classification systems, thesauruses (thesauri) and authoritative lists of words (often called controlled vocabularies) which indexers and cataloguers use to establish semantic relationships or subject concepts.

Some systems, for example the Universal Decimal Classification system (UDC) and Dewey Decimal Classification system (DDC), attempt to classify all areas of knowledge. Other systems cover specific subject areas such as law (MOYS Classification) and medicine (MeSH — Medical Subject Headings). The Library of Congress Subject Headings (LCSH) Listing is the thesaurus used for cataloguing the Library of Congress collections.

A thesaurus is a very detailed classification system. It is alphabetically arranged and generally contains:

- annotations about the usage of the term: for example, **SN** — scope note; **UF** — use for; **USE** — to direct to another term;
- a hierarchy of terms or subjects: for example, **BT** — broader terms; **NT** — narrower terms;
- related terms: for example, **RT** — related terms (synonymous or quasi-synonymous relationships);
- the date showing when the term became part of the thesaurus: for example, **DI** — date of index term;
- sometimes the broadest term of the category (the one at the top of the hierarchy): for example, **TT** — top term;
- sometimes a broad classification code: for example, **CC.**

The following are examples of subject classification schemes:

1. The ***INSPEC Thesaurus*** (Institution of Electrical Engineers).
2. DDC as adopted by the ***BUBL Information Services***, an Internet subject directory.
3. *AustLII*, an index to Australian legal information on the Web.
4. *Yahoo*, an Internet subject directory.

Information retrieval		**Information retrieval system evaluation**	
UF	data access	BT	information retrieval systems
	CD-ROM searching	TT	computer applications
	data querying	CC	C7250
	database querying	DI	January 1969
	document retrieval		
	online literature searching	**Information retrieval systems**	
	retrieval, information	UF	archiving systems
NT	query formulation		databases, online
	query processing		information storage systems
	relevance feedback		online databases
BT	information science		online databases
TT	computer applications	NT	bibliographic systems
RT	bibliographic systems		factographic databases
	CD-ROMs		information retrieval system evaluation
	information analysis		full-text databases
	information storage	BT	information science
	online front-ends	TT	computer applications
	query languages	NT	CD-ROMs
	records management		information systems
	software agents		optical publishing
CC	C7250, C7260		public information systems
DI	January 1969	CC	C7250
		DI	January 1969
Information retrieval languages			
	USE **query languages**		

Figure 4.4 Excerpt from ***INSPEC Thesaurus*** 1991

BUBL Information Services has two separate directories. One is alphabetical, the other — the *Subject Libraries* — classifies Internet resources according to DDC.

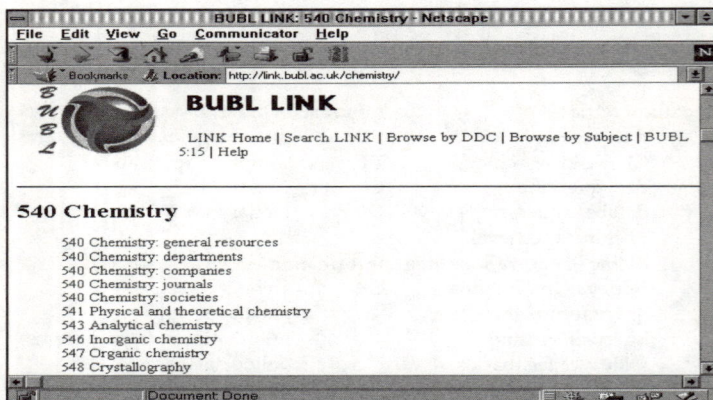

Figure 4.5 **BUBL Link** subject directory — DDC arrangement, 5 June 1998

The *AustLII* (Australian Legal Information Institute) Source Index is not a thesaurus. It categorises Australian Web sites related to law according to their source or 'author'.

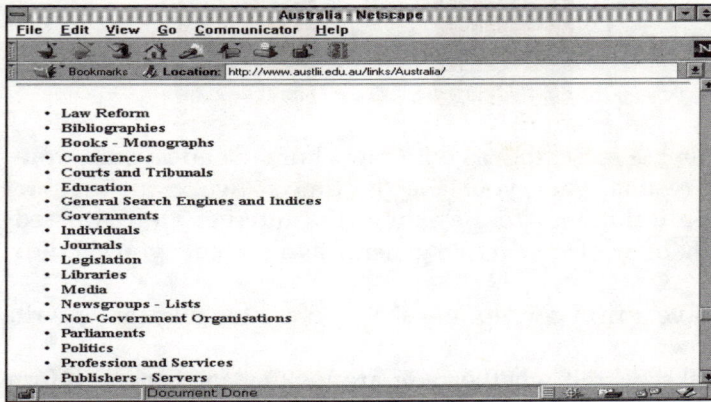

Figure 4.6 **AustLII** Source Index to Australian legal information, 5 June 1998

The **Yahoo** Internet subject directory is not a thesaurus either, but a hierarchical subject classification. Figure 4.7 shows the **robotics** section which is in the **Science: Engineering: Mechanical Engineering** hierarchy.

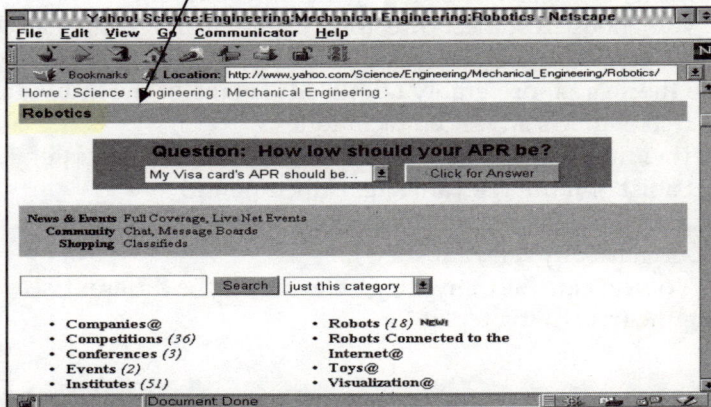

Figure 4.7 **Yahoo** listing for robotics, 5 June 1998

General search strategy

With online searching, as with most human endeavours, you get better results when you take the time to work out a strategy. Specific techniques for searching the Internet are discussed in later chapters. However, in general, as a searcher you should:

1. Have a firm concept of what you are looking for — write it down.
2. Ask yourself whether you are looking for general information or something specific.
3. Decide what type of 'document' you are looking for — Web page, software, Network News.
4. List synonyms for each concept.
5. Select the appropriate tool — Internet, known Web server, database vendor, reference tool.
6. If you want the Internet, select the search engine (something specific) or subject directory (general resources).
7. If you choose a subject directory, use its search engine as the topic you want may be spread across several categories.
8. Do the search, preferably taking advantage of the individual search engine's advanced techniques.
9. Refine the search, if necessary, by modifying the strategy to get a list of more relevant sites/'documents'.
10. Examine the documents by clicking on the URLs listed.
11. Bookmark any relevant site(s).
12. If you do not find anything relevant, try a different search engine (return to Step 6).

5 Internet and Web resources

Overview

Since 1991 when the *NSFNet* lifted its restrictions on commercial use of the Internet, there has been a radical change in the resources available on the Internet. This change is driven by the commercialisation of the Internet environment. No longer is the Internet solely for electronic messaging services and the free exchange of information. The Internet, and more particularly its manifestation as the World Wide Web, is being used more and more as a vehicle for marketing, advertising and conducting electronic commerce, which simply means the buying and selling of goods and services. Table 5.1 shows the change in the use of the Internet over the last twenty years.

Table 5.1 Changes in Internet usage

1970s	1990s
• email • access to freely available information	• email • access to freely available information • advertising • information for sale • 'gated' information services

Much of the 'goods' being sold over the Web is information and many of the 'services' are the provision of gateways to non-public information sources such as proprietary databases, for example those hosted by *Dialog*. Such services are called 'gated services'. These gated services are covered in detail in Chapter 6.

'Free' Web sources vs 'traditional' sources

When do you use the Web and when do you rely on your printed sources or search databases available from online vendors? This question of source selection is still very valid but perhaps should be rephrased: When do you access 'freely available' information and when do you use a 'gated' service? In order to select wisely you have to know what is contained in the information source, how it is arranged and how it can be efficiently accessed. You should treat the Web as just another information source. This means going through the same process of selection you normally do when you use a reference book, a CD-ROM or an online database via a vendor such as *Dialog* or *Ovid Technologies*.

Here are a few rules of thumb:

1. Use 'traditional' sources for older, static information such as government reports published BTW (Before the Web). Much of such 'legacy' information is not converted to electronic format because of expense and other priorities.
2. Use online databases when you know of, or can find one almost certain to contain specific information on your topic. For example, if you need to know specific methods of

managing industrial waste created by oil refining, use the ***Pollution Abstracts*** database.

3. Use the Web for the latest update on constantly changing information such as stocks, weather, current events, train timetables and software releases.

4. The Web is a communication tool and as such may be used by anyone to 'publish' a document or opinion. Therefore many of the sources are not authoritative or lack clues to their authenticity.

5. Try to use the Web sites of organisations that either produce the information you need or are recognised authorities in the field. Here are two examples:

   - For a copy of the software ***Alexa*** that provides information about the value of each Web site you visit, go to the *Alexa* organisation (http://www.alexa.com).

   - For authoritative epidemiological data on **dengue fever** you could try the US Center for Diseases Control — the US Government agency for collecting statistics on communicable and infectious diseases (http://www.cdc.gov).

The challenges of Web searching

The major barrier to finding **relevant** information on the Web is the size of the Web. A recent estimate of the number of documents on the Web is 350 million. The two largest search tools are ***Altavista***, indexing140 million documents and ***Inktomi***, which powers ***HotBot***, ***GoTo***, ***Snap*** and ***Anzwers***, indexing 110 million documents (*Search Engine Watch*, 4 August 1998). No tool indexes the entire Web and each tool may index different documents.

Because of this enormous number of documents each search tool attempts to provide methods of reducing irrelevancies. But the fact remains that most persons using the search tools do not understand the finer points of electronic text searching. They simply type a couple of keywords into the search form and wonder why they are presented with a list of 1 or 2 million Web sites!

Other problems:

- The detection of identical documents is difficult.
- There is no formal way to discover new resources.
- There is a lack of *metadata* (data about the document such as author, date of publication, maintainer of the Web site). For further information on metadata see pages 100 and 164.
- The rejection of irrelevant documents is difficult.
- 'Word spamming' — the inclusion of text designed to 'fool' a search engine into ranking a page as more relevant than it really is — is sometimes done by companies who wish to sell a product and therefore want their home pages to appear at or near the top of a list of search results.
- The indexes created by the search tools are often out of date and the documents are no longer to be found (this is the '404 Error — requested item not found')

Various search tools and other software are attempting to solve these problems, with varying degrees of success. Some of these developments are as follows:

- Duplicate documents can be presented as 'alternate sites'.
- Most search engines now penalise 'spamming' by giving the document a lower ranking.
- Work is being done on metadata standards by the **Dublin Core** (OCLC/NCSA). The standardisation (and application) of metadata to Web documents will provide better methods for retrieving information from the Internet.
- Governments are implementing the use of metadata for their electronic information — the Australian Government's initiative, AGLS (Australian Government Locator Service), will require all Web-based documents to be described with metadata. In the United States there is a similar initiative, the Government Information Locator Service (GILS).
- All the major search engines now index terms in the meta tags, and some use the content of meta tags to 'boost' the relevancy. For example, most search engines rank documents highly if the requested word appears in the title meta tag. However, at the time of writing no search engine allows you to search the contents of meta tags other than the title.
- Many organisations are providing search engine indexing to their Web sites. While a Web search engine's index may contain pointers to some of an organisation's documents, an organisation's search engine may index the entire site, thus allowing you access to all its documents.
- The problem of 'vanishing' Web documents is being addressed by PURLs (Persistent URLs), URIs (Uniform Resource Identifiers) and the *Internet Archive* Project (see Chapter 14).

See *Features of selected search engines*, on page 113, for further details on the developments being initiated by the search tools.

File types and plug-ins

Often you discover the 'perfect' document on the Web, only to find that your browser does not allow you to open it. Instead you get a window like that in Figure 5.1.

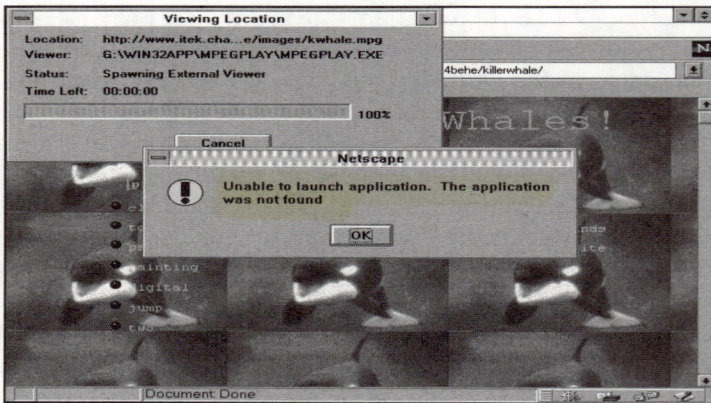

Figure 5.1 A window showing a plug-in is required to open a file

What you need is a 'plug-in'. Plug-ins and helper applications are computer programs the browser calls up to run or display file types encountered on the Internet. Typically a helper application opens a new window *outside* of the browser; a plug-in recognises the file type and automatically runs the program *within* the browser as if it were part of the HTML document.

To install a plug-in or a helper application you need to:

1. Download the software from the Web.
2. Install it in a directory on your computer.

3. Instruct your browser where you have installed it.

Netscape 4.0 comes with plug-ins for many of the sound files, but others you will need to install. This process is explained using the example of one of the file types one encounters often on the Web — the PDF file. This is a file created by Adobe *Acrobat ®*, a desktop publishing software. In order to read a PDF file you need to download and install the *Acrobat Reader* software.

Acrobat Reader can be downloaded from Adobe's Web site (http://www.adobe.com).

Once you have downloaded the software, within *Netscape*:

1. Select **Edit** from the menu bar.

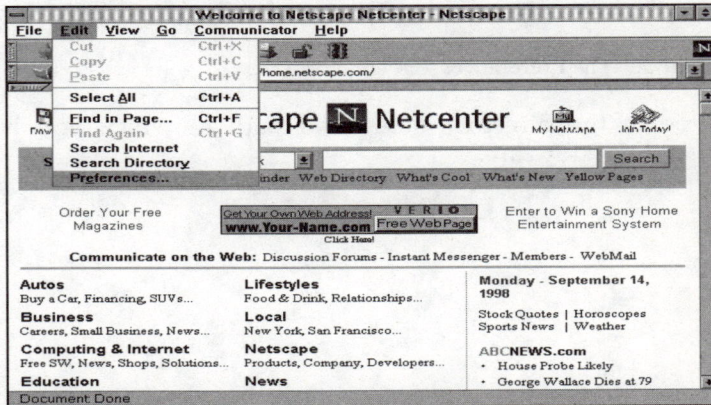

Figure 5.2 **Netscape**'s Preferences

2. Select **Preferences**.
3. Select **Applications,** go to the appropriate application from the list and select **Edit**.

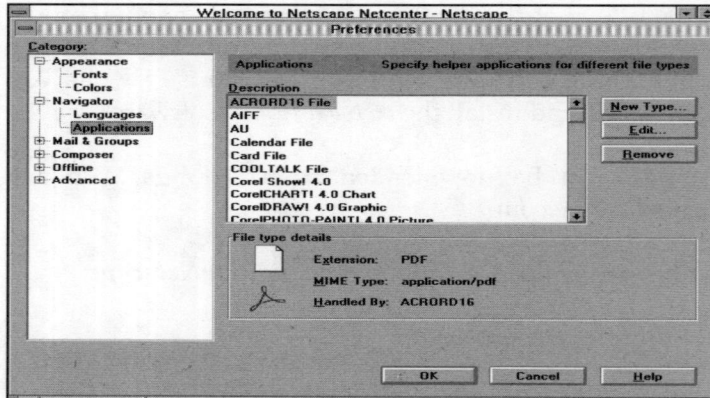

Figure 5.3 The **Preferences** screen in *Netscape*

4. Type in the directory name and path in which you have placed the software.

5. Turn off the box 'Ask me before opening downloaded files of this type' — if this box is not turned off the plug-in will need to be opened outside of the browser before the PDF file can be viewed.

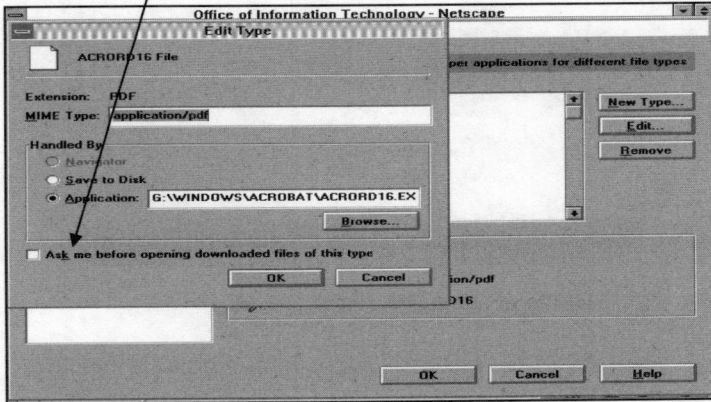

Figure 5.4 Editing the plug-in/application

Once you have completed these steps, when you click on a link to a PDF file, the browser automatically opens the *Reader* for you to view the document. Here in Figure 5.5 is an example of a link to a PDF file.

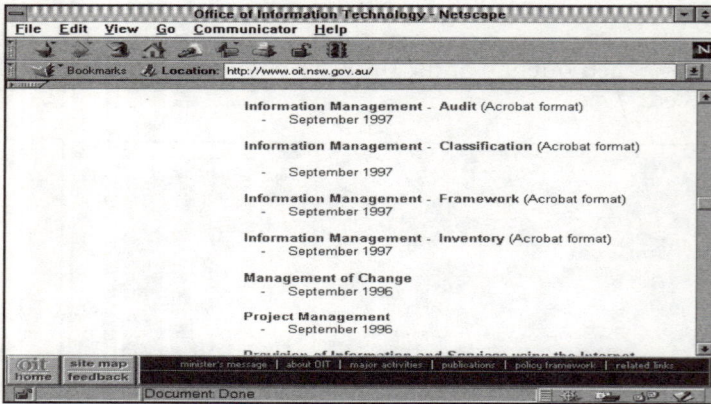

Figure 5.5 A example of a link to a PDF file on the Web

Figure 5.6 below shows the file opened in Adobe's *Acrobat Reader*.

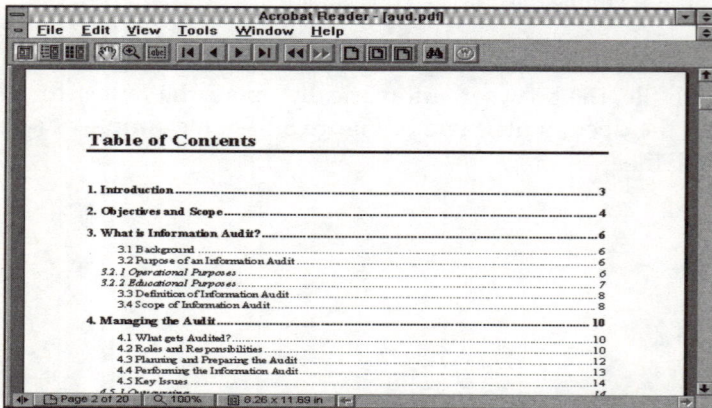

Figure 5.6 A PDF file opened in Adobe's *Acrobat Reader*

To find out what plug-ins are installed on your computer, using *Netscape* **4.0** select **About Plug-ins** from the **Help** menu. Figure 5.8 shows part of the list of installed plug-ins. The information includes type, description, the extension of file it can read, and its location on your computer.

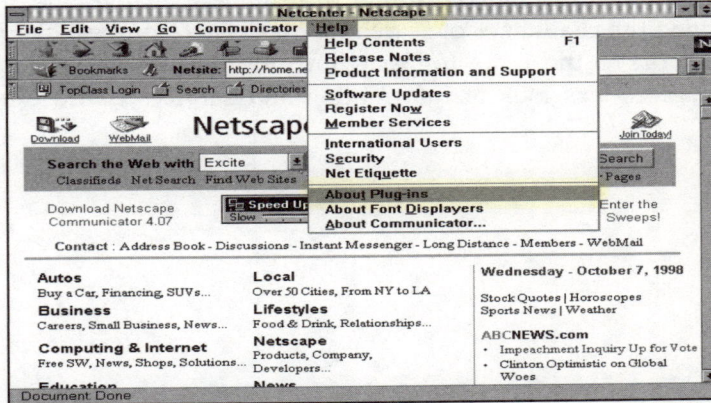

Figure 5.7 **Netscape**'s plug-in menu

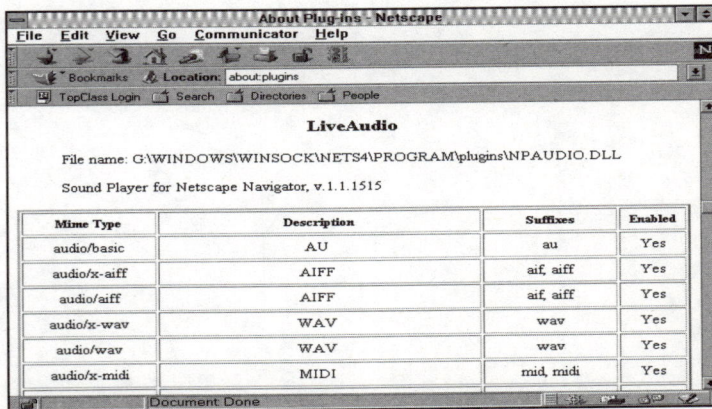

Mime Type	Description	Suffixes	Enabled
audio/basic	AU	au	Yes
audio/x-aiff	AIFF	aif, aiff	Yes
audio/aiff	AIFF	aif, aiff	Yes
audio/x-wav	WAV	wav	Yes
audio/wav	WAV	wav	Yes
audio/x-midi	MIDI	mid, midi	Yes

Figure 5.8 The list of plug-ins installed on a computer

At the time of writing more than 175 plug-ins are available for the current Web browsers.

This chapter has introduced different types of resources on the Web, concentrating on those that are freely available, and has examined the challenges of searching for these resources. Before moving on to the tools for searching for this freely available information, let's look at information and services that are not free.

6 Purchasing information via the Web

Overview

With the growing commercialisation of the Internet, not only is there a vast amount of freely available information, but the Web is being used to access and purchase proprietary information and information services. Some of these services are gateways to online databases. They are often called 'gated' services and they include document delivery services and subscription services.

Gated services

A gateway is a network point that acts as an entrance to another network. With the development of CGI (Common Gateway Interface) scripts, browsers are able to display forms in which a user can input information to send to a Web server. Thus the Web provides free access to the login page of a gated service; the user fills in the login form with his or her password details. The major advantage of accessing gated services via the Web is the simplicity of the browser's graphical user interface (GUI); no longer do you need to use dial-up access via the **telnet** protocol.

The following are three examples of gated services:

1. Access to online databases, such as those hosted by the database vendor *Dialog*. Here are the URLs for some of these online database vendors:

   * *DataStar*   http://dsweb.krinfo.ch
   * *Dialog*   http://www.dialogweb.com
   * *Grateful Med[line]*   http://igm.nlm.nih.gov
   * *Ovid Technologies*   http://www.ovid.com
   * *STN International*   http://www.fiz-karlsruhe.de/stn.html

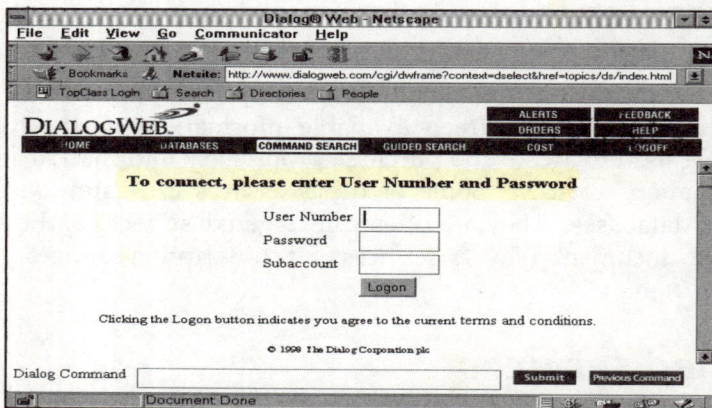

Figure 6.1 The login screen to gated service *Dialog*

2. Many organisations create information such as proprietary databases and research reports which they sell to their customers using a gated service. One such information service is *Australian Business Research* which provides credit reporting information.

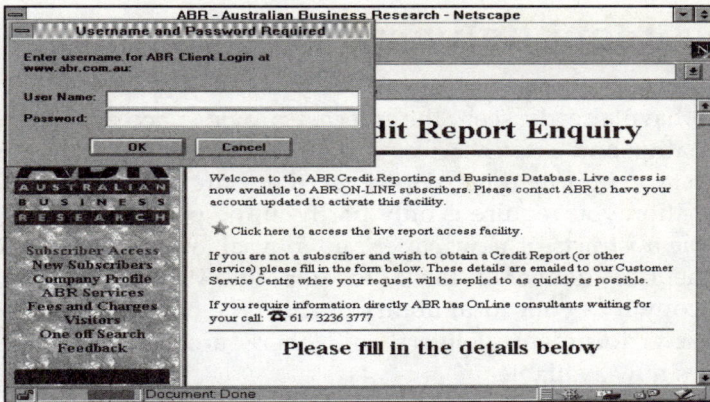

Figure 6.2 Login screen to the gated service *Australian Business Research*

3. A third example of a gated service is one available only to members of an organisation such as a university.

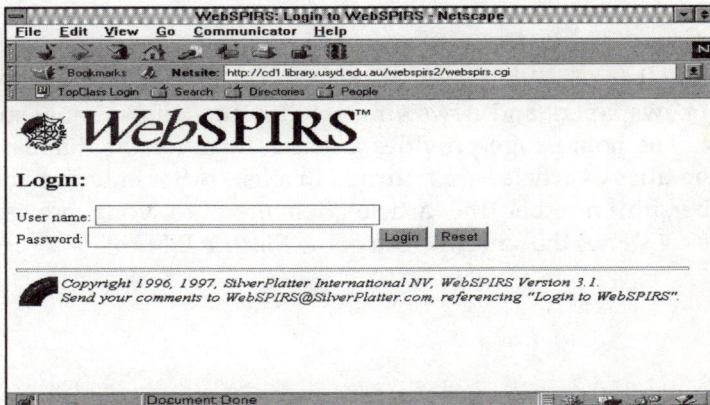

Figure 6.3 Login to a database hosted by the University of Sydney Library

Document delivery

As we have already seen, the Internet provides access to public information and gated services supply their users with their own proprietary information. However there are times when the information you require is only partly in the public domain, for example abstracts of newspaper and journal articles. The entire document is delivered for a fee via the Web (or you can photocopy it at your local library). This type of service is called fee-based document delivery and there are many of these services now available.

Some examples of document delivery services are:

- *Electric Library*   http://www.elibrary.com
- *Northern Light*'s Special Collection   http://www.nlsearch.com
- *UncoverWeb*   http://uncweb.carl.org

The *Electric Library* requires a monthly or annual membership; the annual fee is about $60. It includes in its databases magazines, newspapers and newswires, media transcripts, books and maps. The home page provides a search form for the databases and the titles of articles are returned in a list. After entering your membership number the article 'delivered' to your browser. Figure 6.4 shows the search screen of the *Electric Library.*

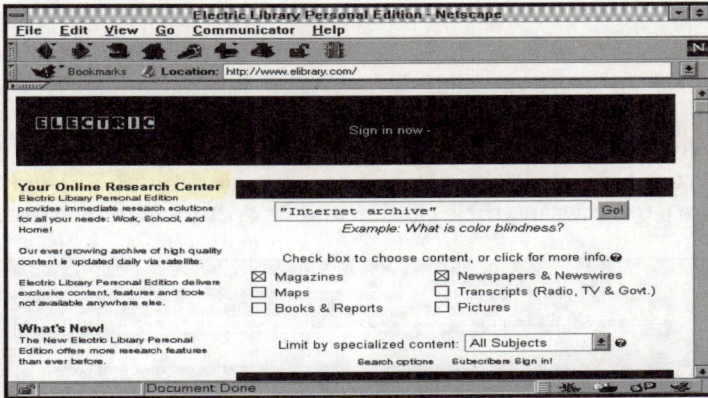

Figure 6.4 Search screen of the *Electric Library*

Northern Light is a general Internet search engine that includes a database of several thousand publications — the **Special Collection**. You may include this collection in your search request, or you may search only this collection. Document delivery requires you have an account and each article costs between \$2 and \$4 (Figure 6.5).

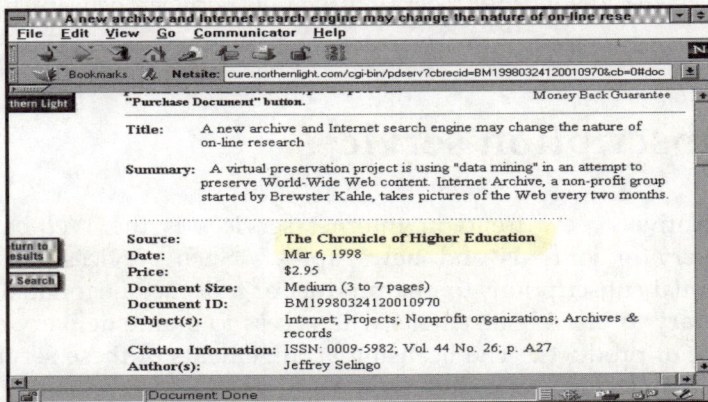

Figure 6.5 Article citation from ***Northern Light***'s Special Collection

UnCoverWeb is a document delivery service that contains a database of current article information taken from over 17,000 multidisciplinary journals. Searching the database via the Web is free and the results give the article citation. Once you have set up an account, any article can be faxed to you for between $10 and $20. Figure 6.6 shows an article citation and its document delivery cost.

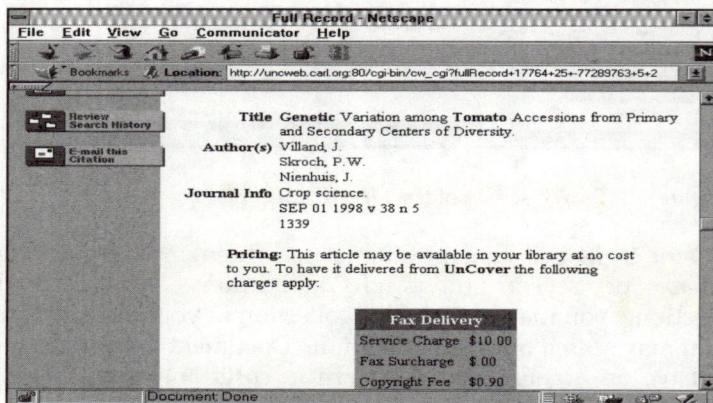

Figure 6.6 **UnCoverWeb**'s journal citation and document delivery charge

Subscription services

A relatively new trend in Internet services is the Web-based delivery of journals and newspapers. Such services can be personal subscriptions to one product or a licence negotiated by a library to provide its clients with access to online delivery of a range of products. The licensing arrangements of these services are complicated and include:

- online delivery if you already have a subscription to the paper-based product;
- a personal subscription to the electronic format;
- online delivery if your institution subscribes to the paper-based product;
- online delivery negotiated by a consortium.

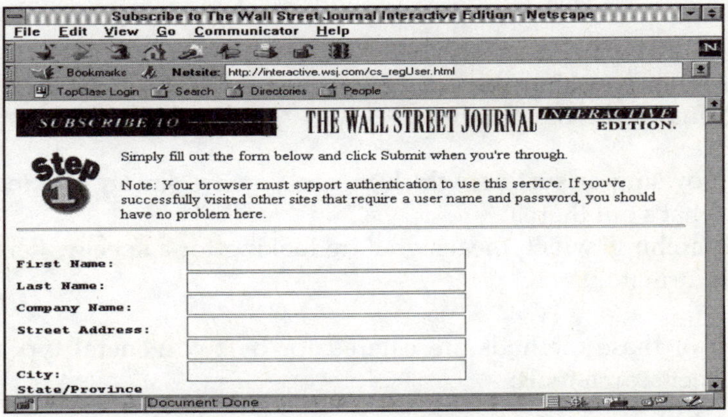

Figure 6.7 Wall Street Journal subscription form

7 Internet search tools

Generally speaking there are two different ways of looking for information on the Internet:

1. browsing or surfing, which means you are simply looking at 'what's out there';
2. searching, which means you are looking for a specific item of information.

Both of these methods are catered for by two general types of Internet search tools:

- *subject directories* for browsing
- *search engines* for searching.

These two types of tools have been expanded, subdivided and combined so that at present the number and variety of the tools available offer opportunities and challenges. Table 7.1 lists the major categories of search tools, how they are created and when you use them.

Table 7.1 Types of Web search tools

Tool	What	How	When
1. People directories	'Whitepages' searching, for example internal telephone directories.	Indexed by robot, or the site developer submits it for inclusion in the index.	When you are looking for email and snail-mail addresses, telephone numbers.
2. Subject directories or guides	Organised, for example hierarchical, faceted.	Manually categorised.	When you are looking for general information about a topic.
3. Search engines	Keyword searching.	'Indexed' by robots, spiders, etc.	When you are looking for specific information about a topic.
4. Multiple access services	Several search engines sequentially accessed.	'Indexed' by robots, spiders, etc.	When you are looking for specific information which you believe may be hard to find.
5. Meta-indexes	Searching several search engine indexes at the same time.	Not an index, but a computer program which searches other indexes.	When you want the highest recall of specific information, that is, an exhaustive search.

Many of the subject directories and search engines are now combining indexing technologies in order to get more relevant search results. Subject directories are incorporating search engines to search their classified databases, and search engines are providing some general categorisation of sites indexed. This combination of capacities is typical in the digital environment and is discussed in detail in the section *Directories and search engines*, pages 89-90.

The commercial services, in particular, are very fluid with buyouts, takeovers and strategic alliances, resulting in the number and variety of the tools available offering opportunities and challenges (see Table 9.3 on page 86 and Table 10.7 on page 114). But whatever search tool you use, you do need to evaluate it. As you use the ones discussed in this book and new ones as they are developed, there are several factors you should consider:

- The accessibility and stability of the tool.
- What does it index?
- How does the mechanism work?
- How are recall and precision handled?
- The presentation of search results.

8 People on the Web

People are information resources

The Internet is primarily a vehicle for communicating with people and organisations; in fact the majority of communication consists of electronic mail. Along with mobile telephones, email is *the* communication tool of the late 1990s. It is used for keeping in touch with friends, inter-office memoranda, contacting sales representatives or politicians, and holding discussions with colleagues or strangers.

Moreover, there is a tendency to rely on people as information sources; most people when they need information, the first move is to ask another *person*. They contact colleagues with similar interests or, if possible, locate a known authority who is willing to speak to them. On the Internet this pattern is replicated using email, newsgroups and listserv discussion groups. But how do you find out email addresses or the names of discussion groups you may wish to join? Let's look first at finding people's email addresses.

Directory services

There is no single listing or directory of email addresses, just as there is no single paper telephone directory for the world. Several commercial and non-commercial directory services are available, but most are not inclusive of any particular region or discipline. They are compiled by a variety of methods. They may be gathered by *robots* (computer programs) from newsgroup postings, or by submission by individuals who are not necessarily the owners of the addresses. These directories are often referred to as 'whitepages' and include directories of email and *snail-mail* (postal) addresses and telephone numbers.

One of the more reliable ways of finding personal contact information, if you know the organisation to which the person is affiliated, is to access the organisation's home page — often there is a link to the internal directory (Figure 8.1). A list of the directories of *AARNet* organisations is maintained by Mark Prior of *connect.com* (http://staff.connect.com.au/mrp/phone.html)

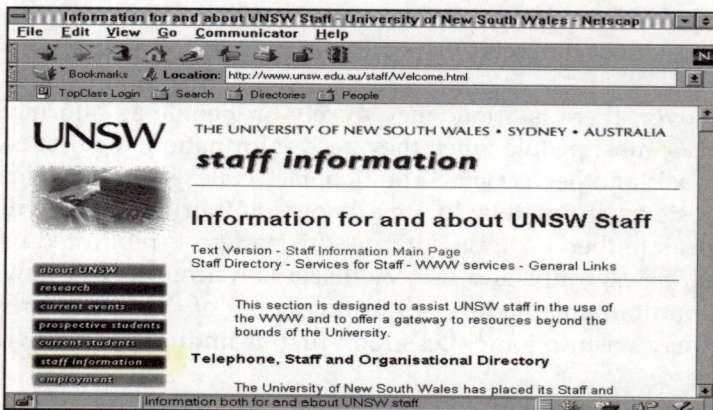

Figure 8.1 Home page giving links to internal directories

The easiest way to get an email address, however, is still to make a telephone call! Here are a few examples of Internet directory services.

Table 8.1 Selected list of 'whitepages' directories

Directory	URL
Australian Directories	http://staff.connect.com.au/mrp/phone.html
Four11	http://www.four11.com
IAF (Address Finder)	http://www.iaf.net
Telstra's Springboard	http://springboard.telstra.com.au/direct/global.htm
Telstra's Whitepages	http://www.whitepages.com.au
Telstra's Yellowpages	http://www.yellowpages.com.au
WhoWhere	http://www.whowhere.com
Yahoo People	http://yahoo.com/search/people
Yellowpages (USA)	http://www.yellowpages.com

You should, of course, compile your own personal email directories and you should consider whether you want *your* email address listed in the public directories. If you decide that you do, these directory services have submission forms on their home pages. For example, Figure 8.2 shows the *WhoWhere* submission form.

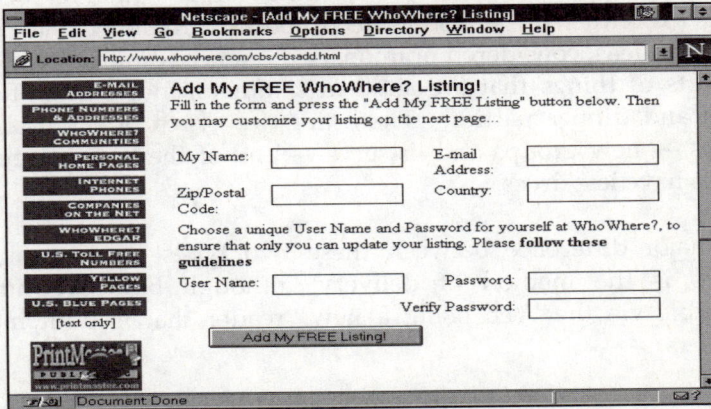

Figure 8.2 Form for submitting email address to a directory service

People directories exercises

Use the services listed above to find the following information:

1. The address of Maureen Henninger, Sydney, Australia.
2. The number of newsagents in Bendigo, in Victoria, Australia.
3. The email address of the Vice-Chancellor of Sydney University.
4. How to contact by email the National Air and Space Museum at the Smithsonian Institution, an educational organisation in the United States.
5. The telephone number of the company Polydrive Industries in Arizona, United States.
6. Is Ross Todd affiliated with the University of Technology, Sydney?

Discussion groups and newsgroups

Often the information you are looking for has not yet been published, either on paper or electronically. Rather it may be still only ideas, considered opinions, experiences or anecdotes — the sorts of things that are aired at seminars, meetings, coffee shops and dinner parties. There are two types of discussion groups — newsgroups and listservs — and of the two, listservs tend to have less dross.

The major difference between these two types of discussion groups is the method of delivery, although both are now accessible via the Web using a news reader that is built into browsers.

1. Listservs — each posting (message) is delivered to the email box of subscribers
2. Newsgroups — each posting is placed on a public server, similar to a bulletin board

Listservs

Listservs originated in the academic community (*BitNet*, one of the earliest networks) but are now 'subscribed' to by anyone with an interest in the subject of the discussion. Although the process of joining a listserv is referred to as subscribing, no fee is involved; your email address is simply added to the list of recipients of the discussion postings.

To subscribe to a listserv you send an email message to the owner of the listserv. In the body of the message you send a message such as **subscribe listserv_name firstname lastname** or **subscribe listserv_name your_email_address**.

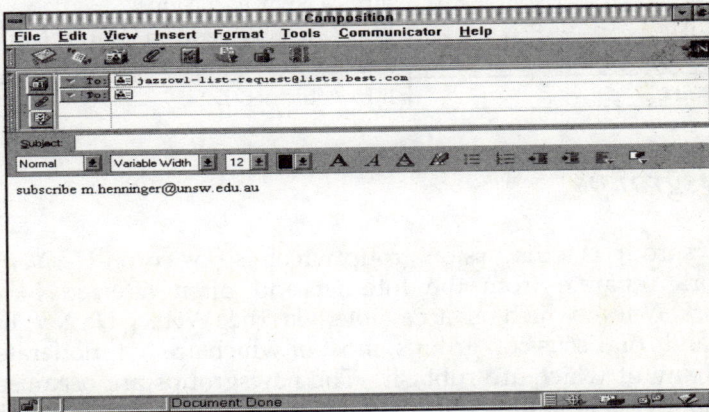

Figure 8.3 Subscribing to a listserv

To stop receiving postings, you 'unsubscribe' by sending a message such as **unsubscribe listserv_name first name lastname** or **unsubscribe listserv_name your_email_address** to the listserv owner.

It is important to read the listserv instructions you receive as an email once you have successfully subscribed. These instructions tell you to what email address you send your postings, and this is generally not to the listserv owner. To post a message to a listserv you simply send an email.

Most people hear about 'valuable' listservs from their friends and colleagues; however there are directories of listservs on the Internet. These directories, listed either by name or by subject, generally give information about the scope of the discussion and instructions on subscribing. Table 8.2 lists some of these directories.

Table 8.2 Selected directories of discussion groups

Directory of Scholarly & Professional E-Conferences	http://n2h2.com/KOVACS/
Liszt	http://www.liszt.com
OZlists	http://www.gu.edu.au/gint/ozlists/ozlists_home.html
Tile.net	http://tile.net/lists/

Newsgroups

A newsgroup is a discussion group which is posted on *UseNet* (a network separate from the Internet and often referred to as *Network News*) which is accessible via the Web. *UseNet* has thousands of discussion groups, most of which are not moderated and many of which are rubbish. The newsgroups are organised into subject hierarchies, the first letters of which designate the category. Table 8.3 lists some of the top level subject categories.

Table 8.3 Selected top level newsgroup subject categories

• bit	listservs	• misc	miscellaneous
• biz	business	• rec	recreation
• comp	computers	• sci	science
• k12	education	• soc	society

You do not access *UseNet* newsgroups in the same way as you subscribe to listservs. Instead your ISP (Internet Service Provider) copies many of them to their server and you access them by using your browser's reader. In many cases you can now access listservs this way if you do not wish to have the postings delivered to your email box.

Below are the instructions for *Netscape*'s news reader.

1. Click on **Communicator** from the menu bar.
2. Select **Collabra Discussion Groups.**

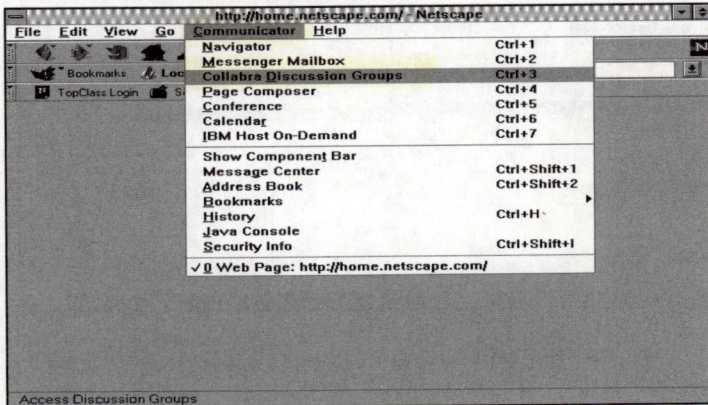

Figure 8.4 Accessing *Netscape*'s mail and discussion groups

3. Fill in the Mail and Discussion Groups Setup. You will need to know the name of your news server — you get this from your ISP.

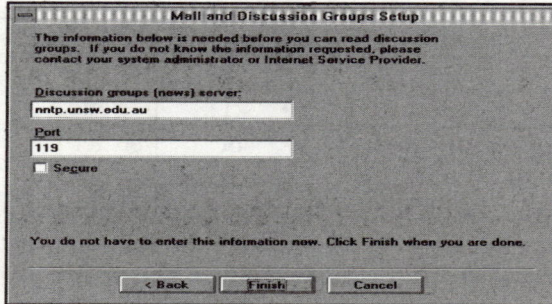

Figure 8.5 ***Netscape***'s mail and discussion groups setup

You are now ready to access discussion groups. From the Message Center select **File**, then **Subscribe to Discussion Groups**.

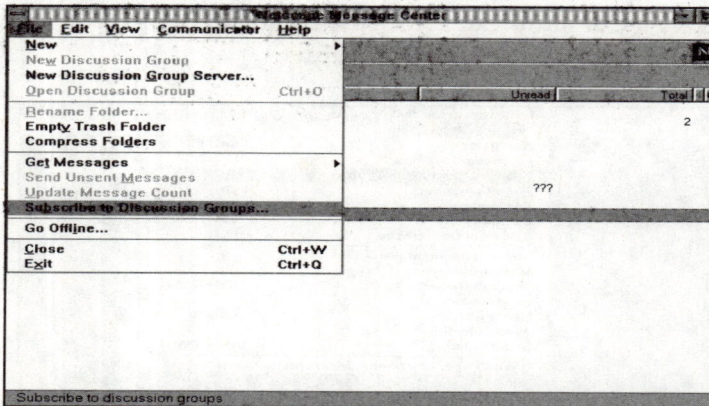

Figure 8.6 Subscribing to (accessing) discussion groups in ***Netscape***

The first time you do this you will need to click on **Get Groups**.

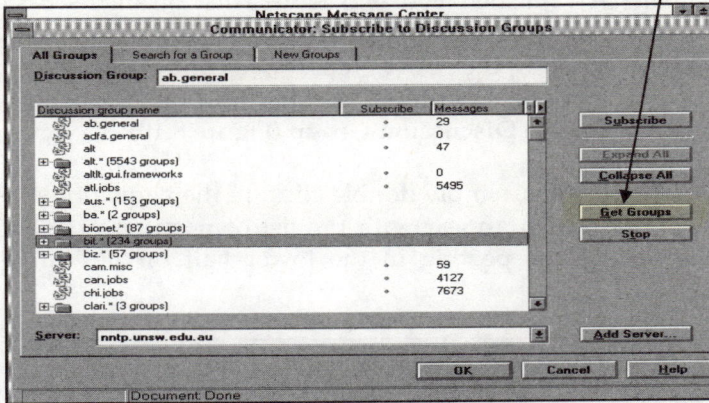

Figure 8.7 The top level of discussion groups subject categories

Work your way down through the hierarchy to find the group you wish to access (or use the built-in search facility), highlighting those you want and clicking on the **Subscribe** button.

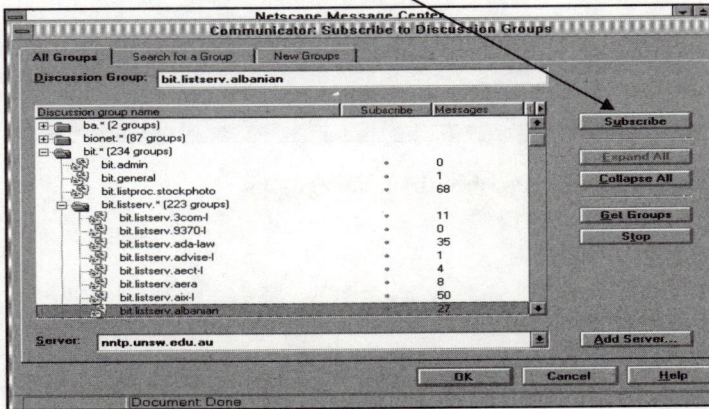

Figure 8.8 List of discussion groups within the **bit** hierarchy

When you have finished you will have a list of all discussion groups you wish to access (Figure 8.9). You can add groups at anytime by repeating the above steps. You can remove a group from your list by highlighting it, clicking **Edit** on the menu bar and selecting **Delete Discussion Group** (Figure 8.10).

To read the postings, simply double click on the name of the list. A new window will appear with the list of postings at the top and the text of the posting in the lower half of the window (Figure 8.11).

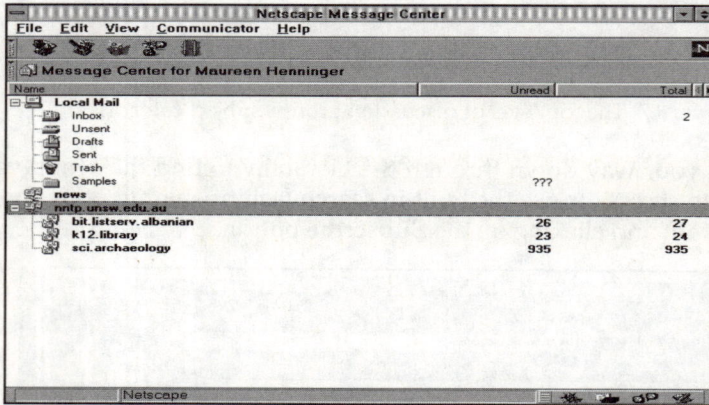

Figure 8.9 List of subscribed discussion groups

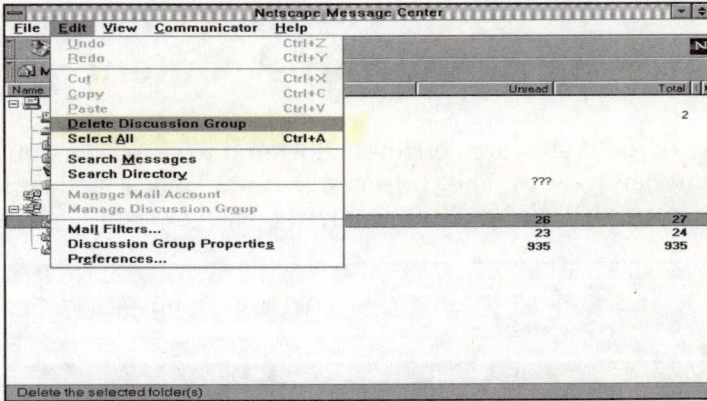

Figure 8.10 Deleting a group from the list

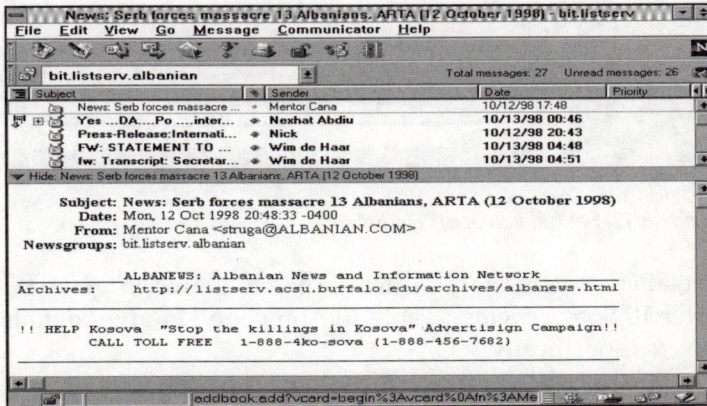

Figure 8.11 Reading postings in a discussion group

Searching newsgroups' content

Many of the Web search engines allow you to search for content within newsgroups and listservs, but the major archives of newsgroups is *DejaNews* (http://www.dejanews.com).

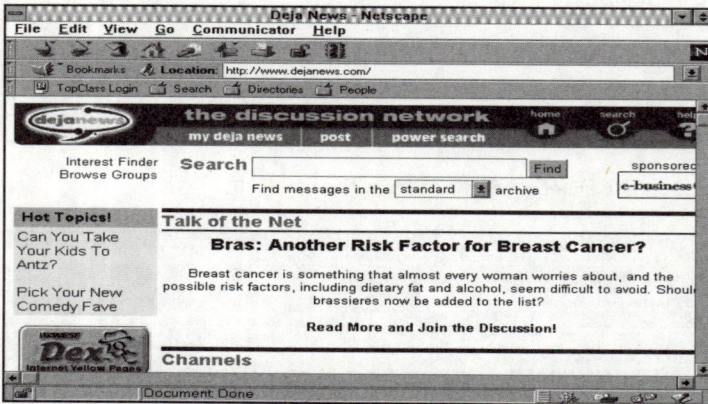

Figure 8.12 Search screen of *DejaNews*

For detailed information on using search engine in general, see Chapter 10 *Search engines*; Table 10.7 on page 114 gives details on *DejaNews* specifically.

Chat, MUDs and MOOs

There are other kinds of Internet communication that allow participants to 'talk' to each other. They are in a sense discussion groups in 'real time'. This means that several persons log into a computer at the same time and interact with each other by typing commands and messages.

The most popular of these is IRC (Internet Relay Chat). A very good source of information about IRC is *IRC Help* (http://www.irchelp.org/)

MUDs (originally Multi-user Dungeon, and now Multi-user Dimension) and MOOs (Multi-user Object-oriented MUDs) are social spaces managed by computer programs in which the participants adopt character names or alter-egos. Most of these MUDs and MOOs are still text-based and may be designed for socialising or for education. A good directory of MUDs and MOOs is *MUD Directory Players* (http://mudconnector.com/mpd/).

9 Subject directories/guides

Overview

There are many subject directories on the Web which attempt to organise the resources on the Internet. They are indexes or catalogues of Web sites arranged according to classification schemes and they may be as simple as an alphabetical listing or as formal as UDC (Universal Decimal Classification), DDC (Dewey Decimal Classification) and the Library of Congress Classification System. Most are broad, generalised categories such as:

- Health and Fitness
- Science and Technology
- Entertainment and Media
- Recreation and Sports

The categories within the classification schemes are created by people (editors). In most cases the creator of a site submits the site to the subject directory for inclusion, and the editors then manually assign the site to one or more categories according to set criteria.

Tables 9.1 and 9.2 give some indication of the variety of subject directories available on the Web, their URLs and their key features. Included here are only general subject directories, developed and maintained by both commercial and non-commercial enterprises. Chapter 11 covers specialised subject directories — **subject gateways**.

Table 9.1 Selected list of subject directories

Directory	URL
A2Z (Lycos)	http://a2z.lycos.com
Argus Clearinghouse	http://www.clearinghouse.net
The Aussie Index	http://www.aussie.com.au/index.html
AustLII	http://www.AustLII.edu.au/links/Australia/Subjects
BUBL Link	http://www.bubl.ac.uk
eBLAST	http://www.eblast.com
Galaxy	http://www.einet.net/galaxy.html
LookSmart	http://www.looksmart.com
Magellan	http://www.mckinley.com
Snap	http://www.snap.com
WWW Virtual Library	http://www.vlib.edu
This is Australia	http://springboard.telstra.com.au/index.html
Yahoo	http://www.yahoo.com

Criteria for inclusion

Each subject directory service has its criteria for accepting submissions. Some are more stringent than others. See Table 9.2 below for some examples.

Table 9.2 Examples of subject directories' selection criteria

Subject directory	Selection criteria
Argus Clearinghouse <http://www.clearinghouse.net/ratings.html>	• Level of resource description • Level of resource evaluation • Guide design • Guide organizational schemes • Guide meta-information
eBlast <http://www.eblast.com/about/faq.html>	• Depth and accuracy • Credentials and authority of author or publisher • Frequency of revision • Quality and effectiveness of presentation
OMNI <http://omni.ac.uk/agec/evalguid.html>	• Scope • Accuracy • Provenance of information • Currency • Uniqueness
Yahoo	• User submission

Features of selected subject directories

Details of some of the Internet subject directories are listed in Table 9.3. This is not an exhaustive list of the available subject directories, nor of their features. The features included are:

- the provenance or ownership of the service;
- what resources are included;
- how the directory is structured;
- any specific value added to the service.

These features change constantly and the most up-to-date information about any Internet search tool is obtained from its Web site. When you get to the site, look for FAQs, guides and other items 'about' what you are looking for, for example 'About this Company'.

Table 9.3 Features of selected subject directories

Directory	Who	What	How	Value-added
Argus Clearinghouse	Previously Clearinghouse for Subject-oriented Internet Resource Guides from the University of Michigan.	Internet resources guides (bibliographies) which have hypertext links. Sites rated by 1 to 5 checks.	Broad categories such as Art, Business, Education, Medicine; alphabetical within categories.	• Stringent rating system (rating done only once a year). • Incorporates a search engine.
AustLII	Australasian Legal Information Institute, jointly operated by the Faculties of Law at the University of Technology, Sydney and the University of New South Wales.	Australian legal information such as consolidated Commonwealth, NSW & ACT Acts & Regulations, Court decisions and special collections, for example NSW Law Reform Commission Reports.	• Hierarchical arrangement. • Source index. • Subject index. • Alphabetical listing of other legal indices.	• Search engine. • World legal material.
BUBL Link	UK Office for Library and Information Networking, Joint Information Systems Committee, (Higher Education Funding Councils of England, Scotland and Wales)	Originally strong Library and Information slant, now subjects of interest to the research and academic communities.	• Alphabetical. • DDC. • Volunteer effort from subject specialists all over the country.	• Search engine for *BUBLLink* as well as the Web. • Annotations about sites. • Subject tree. • Weekly updates.

(cont. next page)

Table 9.3 Features of selected subject directories

Directory	Who	What	How	Value-added
eBLAST	Created by Encyclopaedia Britannica, originally *eBIG* then relaunched in mid-1998.	• Large subject-specific editorial staff. • Individual site submissions for review. • Sites rated by 1 to 5 stars.	Broad categories of topics such as Health and Medicine, Philosophy and Religion. Some sections classified using standard thesauri.	• Advanced search — eg. by rating or subject. • Search can be extended to include *AltaVista* listings. *Best of the Web* — 5 star sites. • *Special Kids* category. • Site statistics and related links provided by *Alexa*.
Galaxy	Formerly EINet's *Galaxy*, now owned by TradeWave.	Individual site submissions for review. Anticipating submissions will go into database for immediate searching while waiting for review.	Broad categories of topics such as Medicine, Education. 'Galaxy Pages'—collection of references..	• *See also* references at specific subject level. • Incorporates a search engine which allows searching the index of each of the collections. • Links to other subject directories, particularly to *WWW Virtual Library*.
LookSmart	Originally a subsidiary of Readers Digest but now a separate company.	Individual site submissions for review. Searchable listings tap into *AltaVista*.	Broad categories of topics such as Reference and Education. Four levels in the hierarchies.	Incorporates a search engine which searches the Web, People, Discussions, and Shopping sites.

(cont. next page)

Table 9.3 Features of selected subject directories

Directory	Who	What	How	Value-added
Lycos A2Z	Very early search engine developed at Carnegie Mellon. *A2Z* subject directory introduced early 1996.	Individual site submissions.	Broad categories such as Arts, Business, Education, Science. Hierarchical structure.	• Links to related sites.
Magellan	The McKinley Group, Inc., acquired by *Excite* in 1996.	Reviewed sites.	Broad categories such as Arts, Business, Entertainment, Law. One level of sub-categories.	• Each site is reviewed. • Incorporates a search engine tapping into *Excite*'s listings. • Gives 'greenlight' rating to sites — for general viewing.
Snap	Owned by C|Net Inc. and launched in late 1997.	Individual submissions for review.	16 broad categories such as Art & Humanities, Science & Technology. Hierarchical listing with many levels. Individual listings arranged alphabetically by title.	• Short annotations describing site highlights. • Incorporates a search engine, including an advanced search.
WWW Virtual Library	Developed by CERN (European Particle Physics Laboratory). Now maintained by volunteers and hosted by Stanford University.	A 'distributed subject catalogue'. Each subject listing is maintained by editors around the world.	Hierarchical listing. Alphabetical subject listing, with some cross-references.	• Annotations and cross-references. • Arrangement by service type.
Yahoo	Developed by students at Stanford University, now an independent company.	Based on user submissions.	Broad subject categories with a hierarchical or faceted structure.	• Incorporates a search engine. • Search can be executed in other search engines.

Directories and search engines

When search engines were developed it was assumed that by indexing every word in a document their relevance ranking algorithms would produce very good results. As we have noted in the overview of full-text searching, this is not always true. By 1994 the search engines began to introduce broad general subject areas such as sport and health. By 1996 these were being touted as 'subject channels'. Neither of these services included any hierarchical levels of specificity. By 1998 the search engines added commercial subject directories, giving them prominence in order to counteract users' overly-broad searches. For example both *AltaVista* and *HotBot* have negotiated contracts with *LookSmart* for directory listings. Figure 9.1 shows *HotBot*'s search page giving prominence to its broad subject channels.

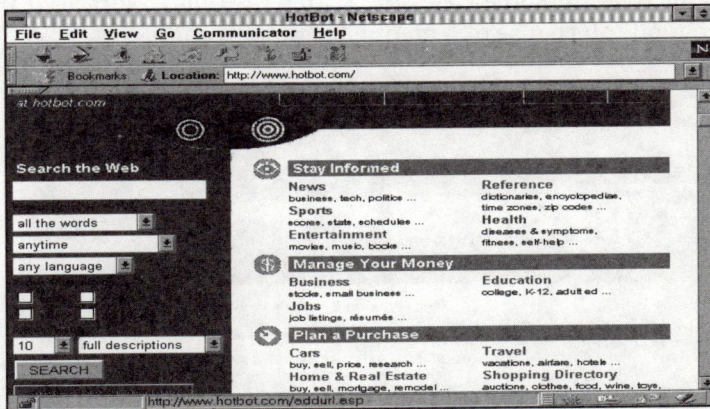

Figure 9.1 *HotBot*'s search page with its broad subject channels

The Health channel is shown in Figure 9.2 with the **More Health Sites** the entry point to *LookSmart.*

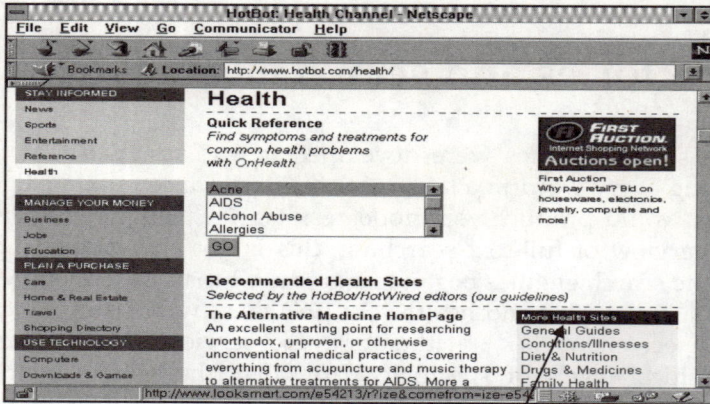

Figure 9.2 **HotBot**'s entry point to **LookSmart**'s health listings

Conversely, subject directories have added search engines to search for items within the directory listings, making searching very effective. In some cases the search also may be passed out to a general Internet search engine for more results.

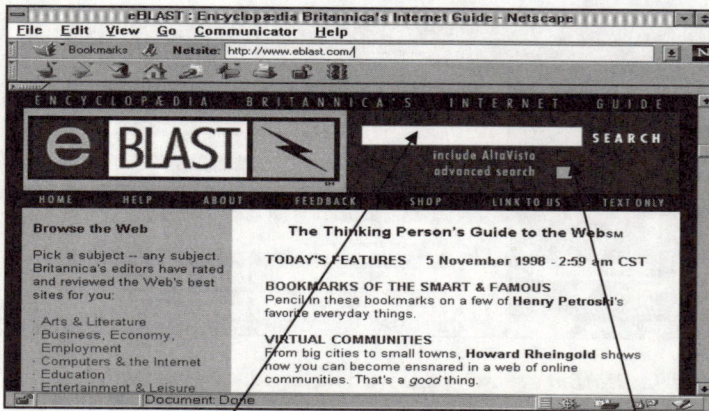

Figure 9.3 **eBlast**'s search engine and facility for including **AltaVista** listings

Subject directories exercises

After doing these exercises you will realise that each of these subject directories (and all the others on the Web) have biases, varying depths of coverage, and advantages and disadvantages. You should become acquainted with many of them.

If you have a specific area of interest, you should monitor the most appropriate subject directories and, following the sites indexed, create your own subject directory. This is covered in Chapter 15.

1. Using *Galaxy*'s subject directory, find general pages on **engineering**. (Note that you can now choose different branches of engineering.) Compare this listing with that of *Yahoo*. What are the major differences?

2. Using *Lycos*'s subject directory *A2Z* choose **Health & Medicine — Illnesses & Disorders.** Find Web sites for **arthritis.** Choose a site about **rheumatology** in children (paediatric) and find related sites, using this value-added feature.

3. **International elections** is a narrower term of **politics** in the subject directory *LookSmart.* What is the complete hierarchy above **International elections**? What is the complete hierarchy for **International elections** in the subject directory *Snap*? Are the listings the same?

4. *Magellan* provides lists of reviewed sites. Examine this directory service for items on **accounting**. How extensive do you find this?

5. Use the *WWW Virtual Library*'s alphabetical listing to find a subject directory on **Aboriginal Studies**. Who is the editor of this subject directory?

10 Search engines

Overview

There are dozens of search engines to help you find information on the Internet. The major difference between search engines and subject directories occurs in the way each is created. As already described, the subject directories are created by people. However, search engines are created by computer programs (called robots or spiders) which move through the Web collecting keywords. These keywords are entered into a full-text index — technically an inverted index that provides pointers to all documents that contain the keywords. It must be noted that most of the search engines, *InfoSeek* being an exception, use a technique of stop words, words such as *or, an, the,* that are not searchable — that is, the search process for these words is stopped. It is this index that is searched when someone types a word or words into a search form and activates the search button. Figure 10.1 shows a search engine with a keyword entered into the search form

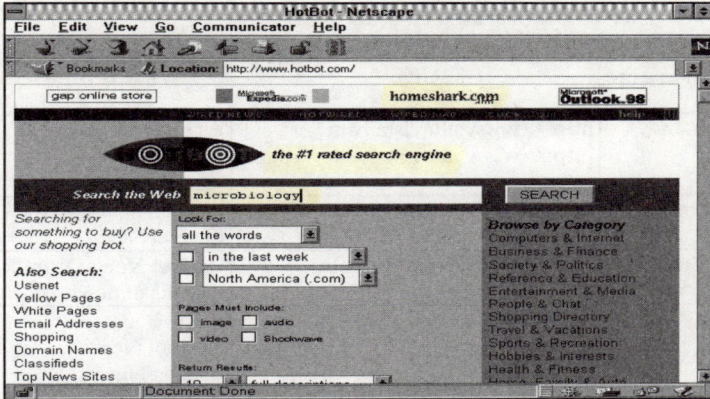

Figure 10.1 Example of a simple search form (*HotBot*)

Search forms differ from one engine to another and ease of use varies, but in general the on-screen directions are not difficult to follow. Some of the more popular search engines and their URLs are listed in Table 10.1.

Table 10.1 Selected list of search engines

Search engine	URL	What is indexed
AltaVista	http://www.altavista.com http://www.altavista.yellowpages.com.au	Web UseNet News
Anzwers	http://www.anzwers.com.au	Web UseNet News
DejaNews	http://www.dejanews.com	UseNet News (approx. 12 months of news)
Excite	http://www.excite.com	Web Current News UseNet News
GoTo	http://www.goto.com	Web Discussion Lists
Hotbot	http://www.hotbot.com	Web UseNet News
InfoSeek	http://www.infoseek.com	Web UseNet News Menu for other collections, e.g. News Wires
Lycos	http://www.lycos.com	Web Reviewed sites Sound and graphic sites
Magellan	http://www.mckinley.com	Web Reviewed sites
Northern Light	http://www.nlsearch.com	Web Special journal collection
WebCrawler	http://www.webcrawler.com	Web Reviewed sites
WebWombat	http://www.webwombat.com.au	Web sites in Australia and New Zealand

The search results are presented to you as a list of sites which have been ranked in order of relevance and depend on the presence or absence of the keyword(s) you have requested. See Figure 10.2 for the first three sites listed by *HotBot* for the search on 'microbiology' shown in Figure 10.1. All the search engines rank the sites for relevance; in the case of *HotBot*, the ranking of the sites is explicit, as a percentage.

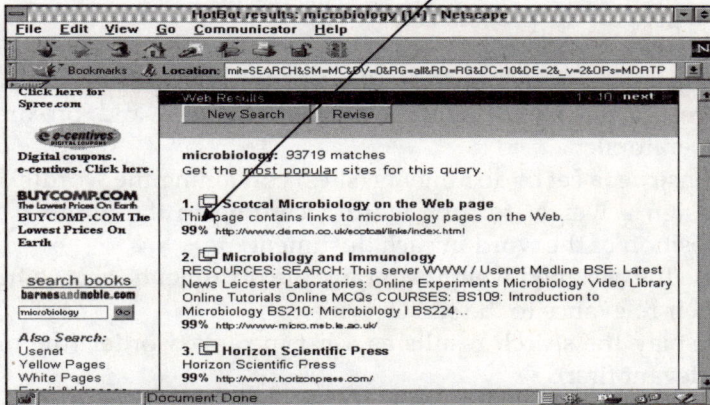

Figure 10.2 Results of search for 'microbiology' (*HotBot*, August 1998)

Relevance and ranking

Search engines are statistically based retrieval programs that determine the relevance and ranking of documents by using algorithms or formulae to select sites in response to a search request. The algorithm differs according to each search engine, but in general the process is to:

1. match the search word(s) to the words in the index;
2. process the search syntax (phrases, Boolean and proximity operators);
3. construct a set of documents (sites) containing the word(s);
4. assign a weight to each word according to the number and position of the word in each document;
5. use the assigned weights to rank the documents, according to their relevance to the search syntax;
6. display the search results as a list in ranked order (the most relevant first).

The weighting or relevance criteria differ according to the search engines, although *Anzwers*, *GoTo*, *HotBot* and *Snap* search engines all use the *Inktomi* index and search technology developed by the University of California, Berkeley. However they are all based on the presence of requested word(s) in the index and on **where** in the document they occur.

The common order of importance of relevance criteria are:

1. the word(s) present in the title;
2. the number of times word(s) are present in the first part of the document;
3. the word(s) present in meta-tag;
4. the word(s) present in a short document often have more weight than the same words in a long document;
5. the number of times word(s) are present in entire document.

However, it must be stressed that even if an individual search engine does use all of these criteria, it does not necessarily place them in this order of importance. Most search engines provide information in their FAQs or search guides about their relevance and ranking criteria. For example:

* *HotBot* specifies the criteria of the word in the title, the word in meta-tags, word frequency and the document length.
* *InfoSeek* specifies the word in the title, the word in meta-tags or the first 200 words, word frequency and uncommon words.
* *AltaVista* specifies the word in the title, the word in meta-tags, the word in the first lines of the document and word frequency.
* *Lycos* specifies the word in the meta-tags (title and heading), the word in the first part of the document.
* *HotBot* and *InfoSeek* use the words in the **content** meta-tag as 'relevancy boosters'.

What is indexed?

'...because these search engines search in different ways and search different parts of the Internet, doing the same search using different search engines will often give you wildly differing results...try out a number of the search engines, and understand that the Internet and the search engines are changing daily' (Eagan and Bender, 1996).

It has already been mentioned that when you do the same search on several different search engines, the results are likely to differ, both in the sites listed and in the ranking of those sites. Figure 10.3 shows the results of a search on 'microbiology' using the search engine *WebCrawler*. Compare these results with the search done on *HotBot* (Figure 10.2).

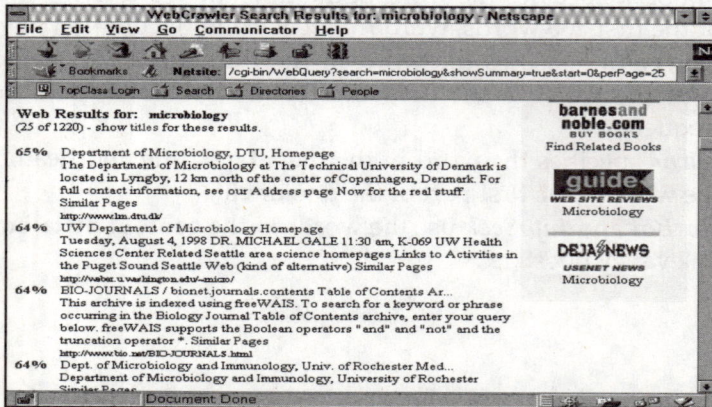

Figure 10.3 Results of search for 'microbiology' (*WebCrawler*, 10 August 1998)

Table 10.2 gives some of the indexing and ranking criteria used by some of the more popular search engines.

Table 10.2 Indexing and ranking criteria used by some search engines, based on *Search Engine Watch*, http://searchenginewatch.com/features.htm (4 August 1998)

Search engine	Content indexed	Meta-tag indexed	Depth of indexing	Popularity indexing	Index freshness	Meta-tag relevancy booster	Popularity ranking
AltaVista	Full-text	Yes	No limit	No	1 day - 1 month	No	No
Anzwers	Full-text	Yes	No limit	Yes	1 day - 2 weeks	Yes	No
DejaNews	Full-text	Not applic.	Not applic.	Not applic.	Daily	N/A	Not applic.
Excite	Full-text	Yes	No limit	Yes	1-3 weeks	No	Yes
HotBot	Full-text	Yes	No limit	Yes	1 day - 2 weeks	Yes	No
InfoSeek	Full-text	Yes	Sample	No	1 day - 2 months	Yes	Yes
Lycos	Abstracts	No	Sample	Yes	2-3 weeks	No	Yes
Northern Light	Full-text	No	No limit	No	2-4 weeks	No	No
WebCrawler	Full-text	No	Sample	Yes	Weekly	No	Yes

Explanation of criteria in Table 10.2

- **Content:** the part of the document that is indexed.

- **Meta-tags:** descriptive words, assigned by the site developer, which do not appear on the displayed document but in the metadata (data about the document). Not all documents have meta-tags; you can look at the metadata of any displayed Web document by selecting **View** then **Document source**. Figure 10.4 gives an example of meta-tags assigned to a particular document.

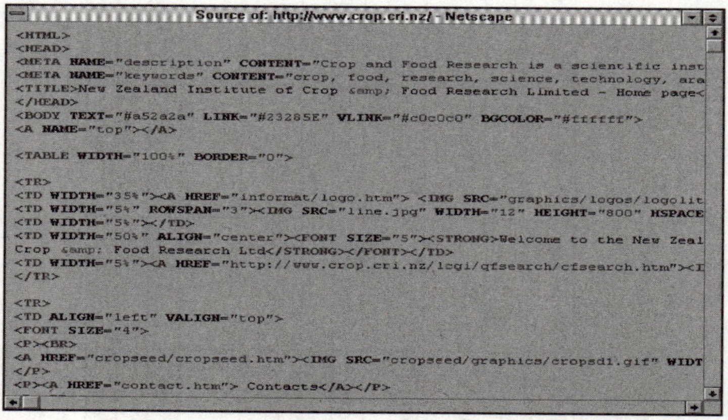


```
<HTML>
<HEAD>
<META NAME="description" CONTENT="Crop and Food Research is a scientific inst
<META NAME="keywords" CONTENT="crop, food, research, science, technology, ara
<TITLE>New Zealand Institute of Crop &amp; Food Research Limited - Home page<
</HEAD>
<BODY TEXT="#a52a2a" LINK="#23285E" VLINK="#c0c0c0" BGCOLOR="#ffffff">
<A NAME="top"></A>

<TABLE WIDTH="100%" BORDER="0">

<TR>
<TD WIDTH="35%"><A HREF="informat/logo.htm"> <IMG SRC="graphics/logos/logolit
<TD WIDTH="5%" ROWSPAN="3"><IMG SRC="line.jpg" WIDTH="12" HEIGHT="800" HSPACE
<TD WIDTH="5%"></TD>
<TD WIDTH="50%" ALIGN="center"><FONT SIZE="5"><STRONG>Welcome to the New Zeal
Crop &amp; Food Research Ltd</STRONG></FONT></TD>
<TD WIDTH="5%"><A HREF="http://www.crop.cri.nz/lcgi/qfsearch/cfsearch.htm"><I
</TR>

<TR>
<TD ALIGN="left" VALIGN="top">
<FONT SIZE="4">
<P><BR>
<A HREF="cropseed/cropseed.htm"><IMG SRC="cropseed/graphics/cropsd1.gif" WIDT
</P>
<P><A HREF="contact.htm"> Contacts</A></P>
```

Figure 10.4 **Document source** showing keywords (meta-tags)

- **Depth of indexing:** these indicate the depth of indexing. At Level 1, the robot indexes all the words on the 'home page' of a site. At Level 2, the robot follows the links on the 'home page' and indexes those documents, and so on to deeper levels in the site.

- **Popularity indexing:** analyses the number of links to the document and uses this number to determine which page is included in the index.

- **Index freshness:** estimates of how often the search engine updates its index.

- **Meta-tag relevancy booster:** if the search word(s) is in the **content** meta-tag, the page is given a relevancy boost.

- **Popularity ranking:** pages with many links or links from important web sites are give a relevancy boost.

Simple and advanced searches

Most people using these search engines have not heard of Boolean and proximity operators, let alone understand how they work. They are also unaware that there are often two types of searches — simple and advanced. The majority of users simply type one or two keywords into the first search request form they see — the 'simple' search form — and hope to find what they are looking for.

It has already been noted that all the current search engines return results that are based on statistical algorithms. In order to return relevant results to these users, the algorithm for the simple search is designed to present first documents with all requested words in the document title. Thus a simple search often presents you with a reasonable result.

However, in many cases the user can have more control over the search results by over-riding the computer algorithm. This is done by using advanced search searching techniques. Some search engines provide a separate advanced search form, for example, *AltaVista*, *HotBot* and *InfoSeek*. Others, for example *Northern Light* and *WebCrawler*, provide only one search form which allows both simple and advanced search techniques to be used.

The rest of this chapter describes in detail methods to help you have greater control over your search results by using advanced techniques to refine your search requests.

Refining a search

When people look for information, they generally need either:

1. a few highly relevant documents on a specific topic (a narrow search); or
2. an exhaustive search for all available documents on that topic (a broad search).

The sheer number of documents on the Internet (*AltaVista* claims to index 140 million URLs) forces you to use sophisticated techniques to find relevant documents. When a search engine is used, and if only simple keyword searching is done, the number of documents found (known as 'hits') can be enormous. If an exhaustive search is required, you should broaden the search request. If only a few highly relevant documents are required, you should refine the search request by narrowing the search.

Broadening a search

In order to find more documents on a topic, broadening techniques should be used. However, be warned that searching more broadly usually lessens the relevance of the documents. Broadening techniques involve:

- the use of synonyms;
- the use of Boolean OR;
- the use of truncation or 'wild cards', for example **walk*** for walker, walkers, walking, walkabout.

Here is an example of a broad search — find all the available information on **caving** (cave exploration). The search is done on *AltaVista,* and Table 10.3 and Figure 10.5 give the preliminary results.

Table 10.3 Preliminary search results for **caving** (*AltaVista,* 5 June 1998)

Search request	Process	Results
caving	Single keyword in the document	89,490

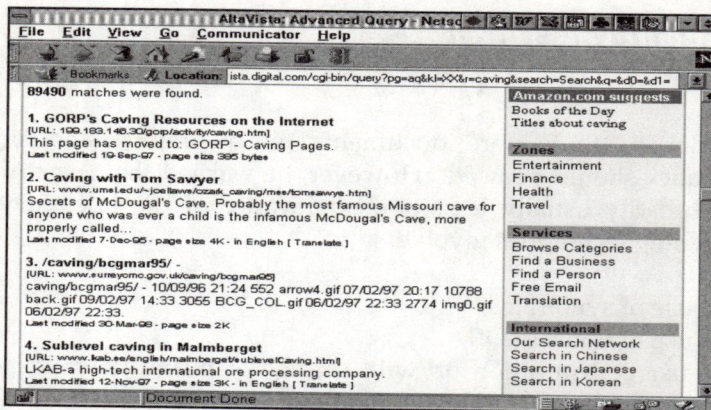

Figure 10.5 Search results for **caving** (*AltaVista*, 5 June 1998)

To find other terms to use, examine some of the documents. In this case I found the technical term for caving is 'speleology' so this was included in the search as well as 'cave exploration'. Table 10.4 and Figure 10.6 show the final results.

Table 10.4 Progressive broadening of a search request (*AltaVista*, 5 June 1998)

Search request	Process	Results
1. **caving**	Single keyword in the document.	89,490
2. **cave exploration**	Phrase in the document.	1,186
3. **cave explor***	Truncated phrase to find any variations in the document: e.g. cave explorer, cave exploring.	2,364
4. **caving OR cave explor***	Any word or phrase variation can be in the document.	3,668
5. **speleology**	Single keyword in the document.	13,031
6. **speleolog***	Truncated keyword to find any variation in the document: e.g. speleology, speleologist.	139,209
7. **caving OR cave explor* OR speleolog***	Any of the words or phrase variation can be in the document.	156,605

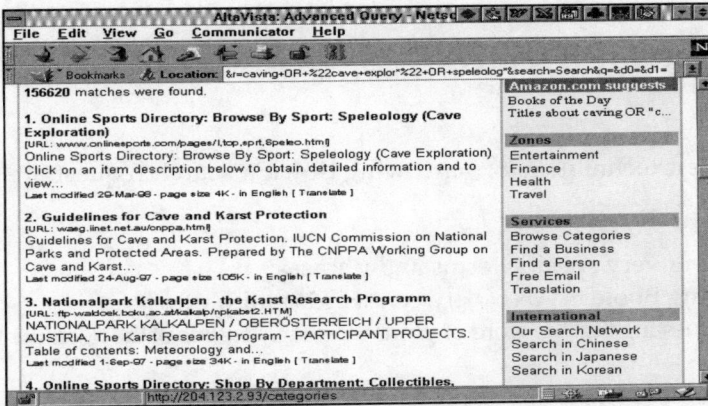

Figure 10.6 Search results for **caving OR "cave explor*" OR speleolog***
(*AltaVista*, 5 June 1998)

In the above examples, I decided not to use the truncation **cav*** as this would return items such as **cavil, Cavillari** and **cavity**. I also decided not to request **cave OR caves** since these words are not synonymous with the **hobby of caving**.

Narrowing a search

The best techniques for narrowing down a search request are as follows:

- using very specific terms and phrases;
- using Boolean AND between words and phrases;
- requesting that the word or phrase occurs in the title of the document.

The following search requests demonstrate refining a search for information on **research in biotechnology** by progressively narrowing down the search requests.

Table 10.5 Search techniques for narrowing a search request

1. **biotechnology research**	'Simple' keyword search.
2. **"biotechnology research"**	'Simple' phrase search.
3. **biotechnology OR research**	Either word must be in the document.
4. **biotechnology AND research**	Both words must be in the document.
5. **biotechnology NEAR research**	Both words must be in the document, and in the same sentence or paragraph.
6. **"biotechnology research"**	Words must be next to each other (phrase).
7. **title:biotechnology AND title:research**	Both words must be in the document title.
8. **title:"biotechnology research"**	The words must be next to each other (phrase) in the title.
9. **title:"biotechnology research" AND Australia**	Adding another concept — the word Europe can be anywhere in the document.

Table 10.6 and Figures 10.7–10.15 show the search results delivered by *AltaVista* which was chosen because it the most flexible in its use of search syntax. The first three search requests use the 'Simple' search option; the other search requests use the 'Advanced' option. (See section *Features of selected search engines*, page 113 of this chapter for the search syntax of a variety of search engines.)

Table 10.6 Results of progressive refining of search requests (*AltaVista*, 20 October 1998)

Search request	Results
1. biotechnology research	8,232
2. +biotechnology +research	367,365
3. "biotechnology research"	8,232
4. biotechnology OR research	5,521,696
5. biotechnology AND research	149,531
6. biotechnology NEAR research	47,362
7. "biotechnology research"	8,815
8. title:biotechnology AND title:research	624
9. title:"biotechnology research"	275
10. title:"biotechnology research" AND Australia	3

Figures 10.7–10.15 show the *AltaVista* search results on October 20 1998. Notice that search numbers 1 and 3 have the same results. To force relevancy in simple searching, a string of keywords are searched as a phrase. Note the different results from the phrase searches — search number 3 (simple search option) and search number 7 (advanced search option). In *AltaVista*'s simple search the phrase must be in the title or top of the document only; in the advanced search, the phrase can be anywhere in the document. Compare Figure 10.7 and Figure 10.12.

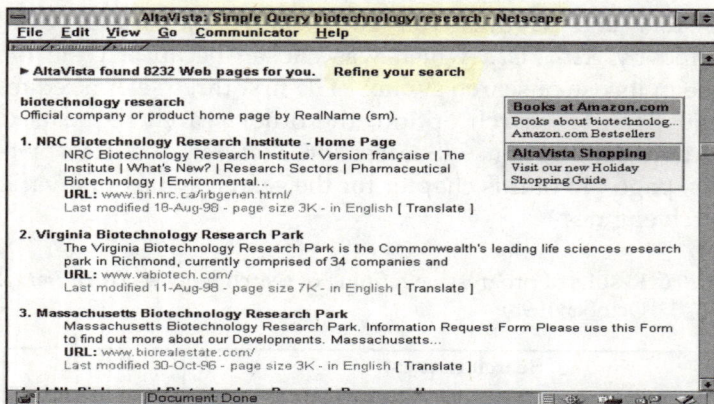

Figure 10.7 'Simple' search request **biotechnology research** (*AltaVista* 20 October 1998)

The 'Simple' search for the keywords **biotechnology, research** (Figure 10.7), is regarded as a phrase. To search for the separate words you need to use '+' before each word (Figure 10.8).

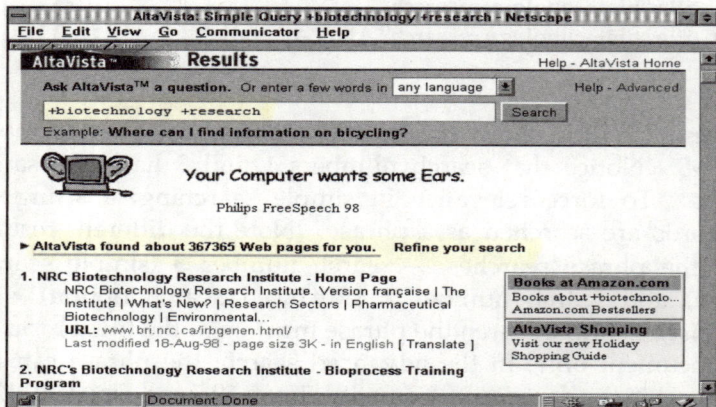

Figure 10.8 'Simple' keyword search request **+biotechnology +research** (*AltaVista* 20 October 1998)

Advanced searching forces *AltaVista* to override its relevancy ranking that give weight to words in the title or top part of the document. Instead the words can be anywhere in the document.

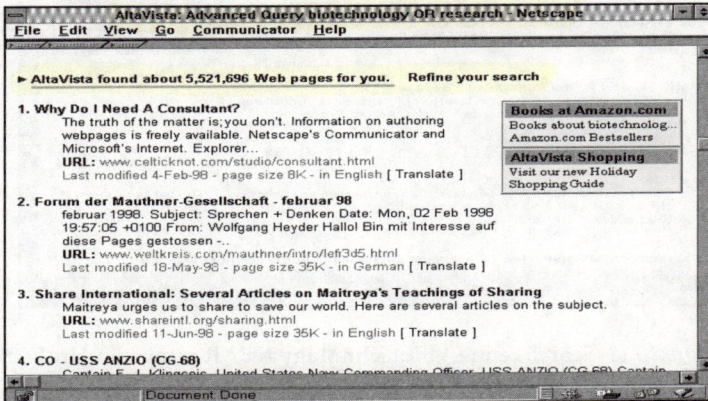

Figure 10.9 Search request **biotechnology OR research** (*AltaVista* 20 October 1998)

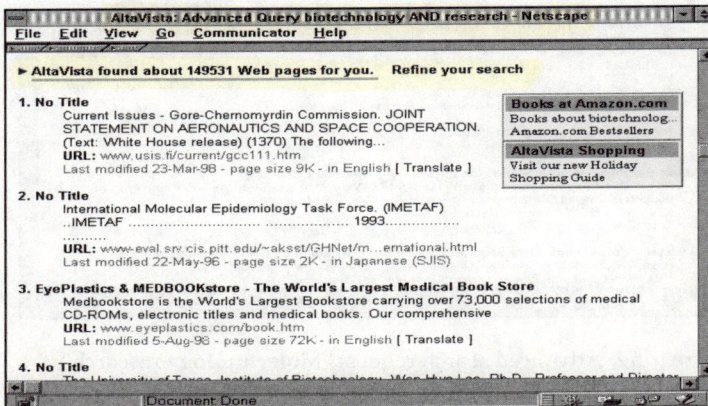

Figure 10.10 Search request **biotechnology AND research** (*AltaVista* 20 October 1998)

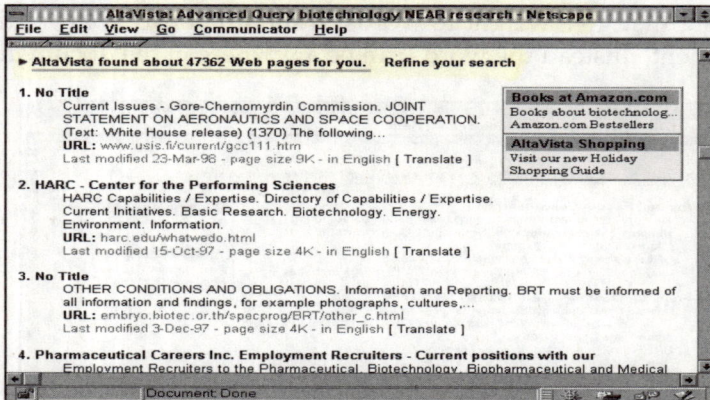

Figure 10.11 Search request **biotechnology NEAR research** (*AltaVista* 20 October 1998)

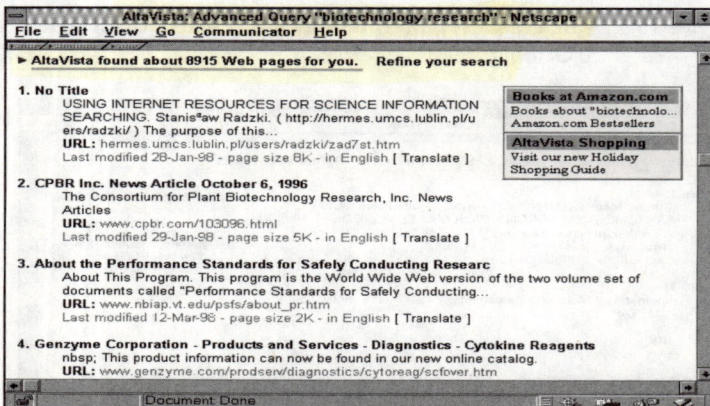

Figure 10.12 Advanced search request **"biotechnology research"**, a phrase (*AltaVista* 20 October 1998)

Notice that in the third item on the list in Figure 10.13, the two requested words are not next to each other.

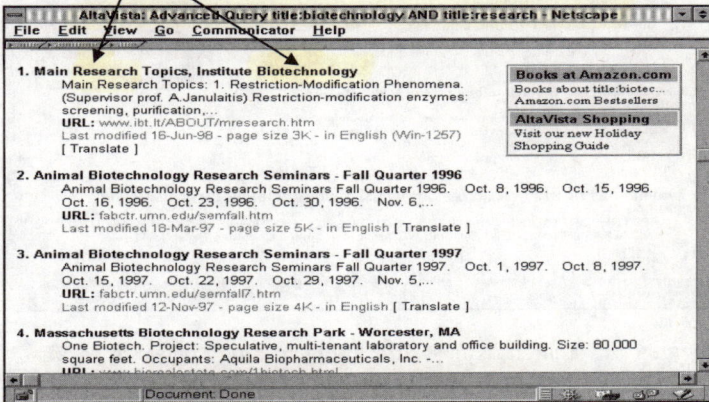

Figure 10.13 Search request **title:biotechnology AND title:research** (*AltaVista* 20 October 1998)

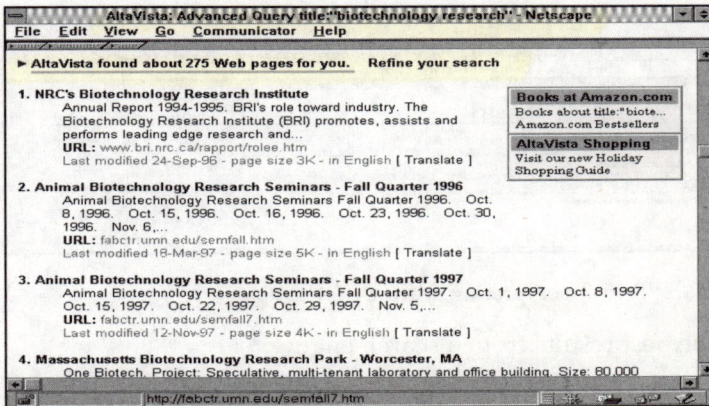

Figure 10.14 Search request **title:"biotechnology research"** (*AltaVista* 20 October 1998)

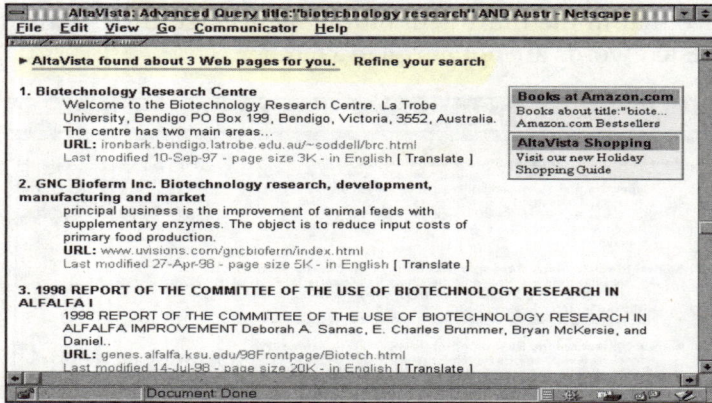

Figure 10.15 Search request **title:"biotechnology research" AND Australia** (*AltaVista* 20 October 1998)

Note: The 'user ranking' feature forces the order in which the results are listed. In Figure 10.16 documents with the word agriculture must be listed first.

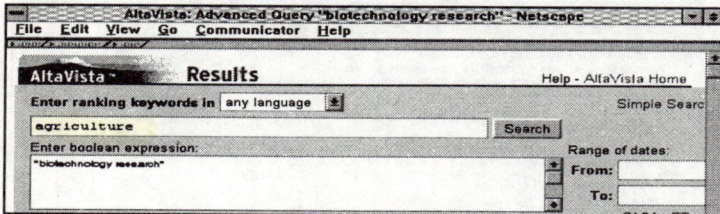

Figure 10.16 'User ranking' feature of *AltaVista*

For the best results from a search engine:

• Use the advanced searching features of the search engine.
• Use the 'help' screen to find out the advanced search syntax.

The next section gives details of the search features of a selection of popular search engines.

Features of selected search engines

Features of some of the Internet search engines are listed in Table 10.7 on the next four pages. This is not an exhaustive list of the available search engines, nor of their features, but shows:

- which Internet resources are indexed;
- which searching techniques are available;
- which search syntax must be used with each search engine;
- other specific values and services available.

These features change constantly and the most up-to-date information about the search engines is found at their Web sites; look for Help, FAQs, and Guides.

Table 10.7 Selected features of search engines

Search engine	Simple search	Advanced search	Boolean	Nested logic	Phrase search	Nested logic	Proximity search	Truncation	Field search	Other
AltaVista	Yes	Yes +-	Yes AND, OR, AND NOT OR is implied	Yes ( )	Yes " "		Yes near (10 words apart)	Yes * Internal truncation, e.g. psych*ist to retrieve 'psychiatrist' 'psychologist'	Yes, e.g. title:	• Advanced search allows customised ranking • Browsing by subject — *LookSmart* • Limit by language • Translations
Anzwers	Yes	Yes *Powersearch*	internal AND, OR with pop-up menu	Yes ( )	Yes " " or pop-up menu		No	No	No	• *Explore* by subject — uses *LookSmart* • 'Wider search' passes query to *HotBot* • Able to modify search • Date ranging • Geographic area • Media type

(cont. next page)

Table 10.7 Selected features of search engines

Search engine	Simple search	Advanced search	Boolean	Nested logic	Phrase search	Proximity search	Truncation	Field search	Other
DejaNews	Yes	Yes	Yes Use symbols & (and) | (or) &! (and not)	Yes ( )	Yes " "	Yes near — can specify, e.g. near 10 (default is 5 words apart)	Yes *	Yes use 'query filter' for author	Can set up a query profile to tailor a search
Excite	Yes	Yes +, - *Powersearch*	OR is implied AND, OR, AND NOT (must be in upper case)	Yes ( )	Yes " "	No	No	No	• Case sensitive (capitalise proper nouns, e.g. **Sydney**) • 'More like this' • *Search Wizard* suggests new words — implied OR, but can use Boolean AND • *Excite News* • *Excite Reference* e.g. addresses, maps

(*cont. next page*)

Table 10.7 Selected features of search engines

Search engine	Simple search	Advanced search	Boolean	Nested logic	Phrase search	Proximity search	Truncation	Field search	Other
Lycos	Yes	Yes — *Lycos Pro*	+, - Custom search AND, OR with pop-up menu	Yes ( )	Yes " "	Yes ADJ, NEAR, NEAR/6 BEFORE FAR	Yes $ Entering ' ' after word, e.g. **bank**. will find 'bank' not 'banking'	Yes title and URL — use a separate menu 'new features'	• 'Related Sites' — Subject Directory • 'more like this' • *A2Z* sites by subject (search) • *Point Review* (*Lycos*'s top 5%) <point.lycos.com>
Livelink Pinstripe (Opentext)	Yes AND is implied	Yes 'power search' form	Internal AND, OR, BUT NOT with pull-down menus	Internal with 'power search'	Yes Simple search pull-down menu	Yes Internal with 'power search' menu	No	Yes Internal with power search' menu	• Newsgroups via *DejaNews* • Japanese, Spanish & Portuguese • Email address via *Four11*
Magellan	Yes OR is implied	Yes +, -	AND, OR AND NOT (must be in CAPS)	Yes ( )	Yes " "	No	No	No	• Owned by, but independent of *Excite.* • '*Green Light Reviews*' — general viewing • Find similiar

(*cont. next page*)

Table 10.7 Selected features of search engines

Search engine	Simple search	Advanced search	Boolean	Nested logic	Phrase search	Proximity search	Truncation	Field search	Other
HotBot	Yes	Yes	internal AND, OR with pop-up menu	No	Yes " " or pop-up menu	No	No	No	• Browsing by subject — *LookSmart* • Able to modify search — 'Search within these results' • Date ranging • Geographic area • Media type
InfoSeek	Yes OR is implied	Yes	+, - use l to force Boolean AND internal AND, OR, NOT with pop-up menu	No	Yes " "	No	No	Yes, title and URL title: URL:	• Groups all pages from one site together • Facility for sub-searching — 'Search within results' • Subject directory— channels

(*cont. next page*)

Table 10.7 Selected features of search engines

Search engine	Simple search	Advanced search	Boolean	Nested logic	Phrase search	Proximity search	Truncation	Field search	Other
Northern Light	Yes	Yes *Powersearch*	+, - AND, OR, NOT	Yes ( )	Yes " "	No	Yes % one character * multiple characters Internal — psych*ist automatic singular and plural	Yes title: URL: pub: text:	• *Special Collection* (Journals, Industry sources) — document delivery for a fee • *Custom Search Folders* — for sorting results
WebCrawler	Yes OR is implied	No	AND, OR, NOT	Yes ( )	Yes " "	Yes ADJ (adjacent) NEAR/n (n words apart)	No	No	• Owned by, but independent of *Excite* • *Select* gives site reviews
WebWombat	Yes	No	AND, OR, NOT	No	No	Yes NEAR	Automatic 'stemming' Gives number of hits for each word	No	• Highlights the requested word(s) in results

Search engine exercises

For each of these exercises, use the advanced features of each search engine, as listed in Table 10.7.

1. Use *HotBot* to find recent (1998) documents on ecotourism. You will find there are thousands of documents. Modify the results to ecotourism in New South Wales. What happens if you use the location option and choose **Oceania?** What are the results if you select the domain **.au**?

2. Find a few up-to-date (last six months), highly relevant documents on diabetes in the elderly.

3. Use *WebCrawler* to find some documents on the health effects of global warming. Can you limit the search to Australia or Oceania? Compare the results with those returned by *AltaVista.*

4. Use *Northern Light* to search for highly relevant information about research on search engines — how many articles? *AltaVista* also allow you to search for words in the title — how many articles do you get? Are the first 5 the same as those on *Northern Light*?

5. Find the paper written by Mary Luria on the control of web advertising. Which search engine did you use?

6. Find a document in Spanish about the persons who disappeared in Argentina during the late 1970s and early 1980s. Can you get an English translation?

11 Search tools by subject

Overview

The Internet began as an academic network for exchanging information. As the technology evolved and the World Wide Web developed, the amount of information grew exponentially; there are now estimates of 340 million documents stored on servers around the world. The proceeding chapters have examined the two major tools for finding required information but neither of these tools can adequately cope with so many documents. The subject directory — a tool that relies on human classification or categorisation of documents, consistently delivers high relevancy. However the trade-off is a low percentage of documents categorised. The search engine, using a computer program is able to index a large percentage of the documents but delivers a much lower level of relevancy, unless highly sophisticated searching techniques are used.

In both cases the search tools cover the entire spectrum of subjects. Of necessity the categories of subject directories such as *Yahoo* and *LookSmart* are very broad, for example *Science*, *Health* and *Medicine*. Search engines are non-discriminating in subject selection, although in an attempt to reduce irrelevancies they are now employing subject channels or indeed installing a subject directory. For example *AltaVista* and *HotBot* use *LookSmart* as their subject directory.

In a perfect world what users want is a tool that indexes every document on a specific subject, thus providing high relevance and total recall of all available documents. As well they want to be assured that the documents are 'good' documents, that is, they are authoritative. Chapter 9 gave examples of the provision of the value-added service of reviewing documents, for example *eBlast, Argus Clearinghouse* and *Magellan*. We will now look at attempts to deliver 'the perfect world'! Tools are appearing which recognise the fact that most users are interested in only one subject at any given time. These tools are specialised subject search engines and subject gateways.

Specialised search engines

The major Internet search engines now provide a facility for searching various types of Internet resources, for example only *UseNet* or only the Web. Using this facility to a certain extent allows you to target certain types of information; in many cases it is used to screen out postings to news groups. Figure 11.1 below shows the menu of resource types that may be searched using *InfoSeek*.

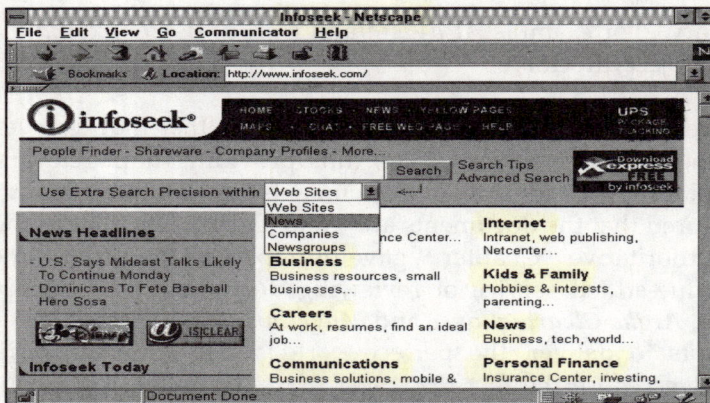

Figure 11.1 **InfoSeek**'s menu for the selection of Internet resource types

Table 11.1 Selected list of specialised search engines

Service	Subject	URL
Ask Jeeves for Kids	Suitable for children	http://www.ajkids.com/
AquaLink	Water plants and animals	http://www.aqualink.com/
DejaNews	Newsgroups	http://www.dejanews.com
MedHunt	Medicine	http://www.hon.ch/MedHunt
News Index	News	http://www.newsindex.com
SportQuest	Sport	http://www.sportquest.com
World Wide Art Resources	Art	http://wwar.com/

Geographical search engines

In many cases you need information which is specific to a country or you wish to limit your search to regional documents. *HotBot* was one of the first general search engines to allow you to do so with its advanced search options.

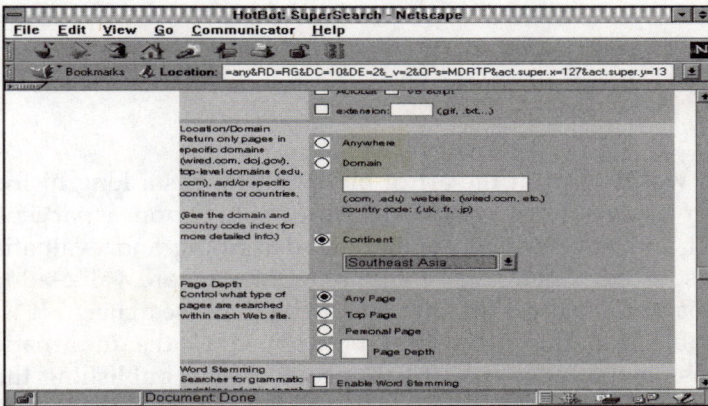

Figure 11.2 ***HotBot****'s facility for limiting by location*

At the time of writing several of the large search tools (for example *AltaVista, Excite* and *Yahoo*) have introduced regional indexes that allow you to retrieve local documents.

There are also a large number of geographic-specific search engines that index only locally held documents. Extensive lists are maintained by *Beaucoup* (http://www.beaucoup.com) and *eDirectory* (http://www.edirectory.com). Table 11.2 provides some examples.

Table 11.2 Selected country-specific search engines

Service	Country	URL
Access New Zealand	New Zealand	http://accessnz.co.nz/
Aladin	Germany	http://www.aladin.de/
Anzwers	Australia	http://www.anzwers.com
UK Index	United Kingdom	http://www.ukindex.co.uk/uksearch.html
VietNet	Vietnam	http://www.vietgate.net/

Subject gateways

In the world of print the art of bibliography has a long history. Subject experts have compiled lists of sources on a particular subject and have added annotations describing and evaluating these sources. Such lists — bibliographies — are value-added information resources and are invaluable for researchers. It was inevitable that this art would be applied to the information sources on the Internet. At first people began publishing their favourite sites (bookmarks) as Web pages, thus providing the first 'webliographies'. And we have already seen general subject directories such as *eBlast* which provide reviewed lists of sources.

Gradually subject experts began creating **gateways** to specific subjects by carefully selecting and annotating sources using rigourous evaluation criteria. These subject gateways are excellent resources that sort the treasure from the trash and in many cases are far more effective than using a general search engine.

The *WWW Virtual Library*, started by Tim Berner-Lee, is the earliest Web directory. It is a 'distributed' catalogue of subject gateways, that is, individual indexes on hundreds of different servers around the world. The subject gateways are maintained by subject experts and Stanford University has taken over the maintenance of the catalogue itself from the World Wide Web Consortium (W3C). These subject gateways are some of the best on the Web.

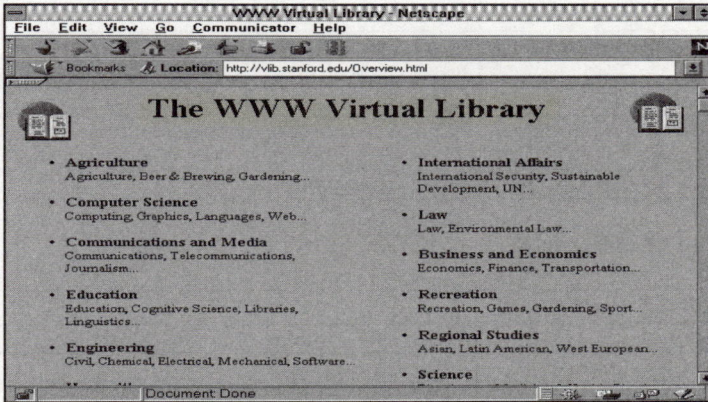

Figure 11.3 The *WWW Virtual Library* catalogue of subject gateways

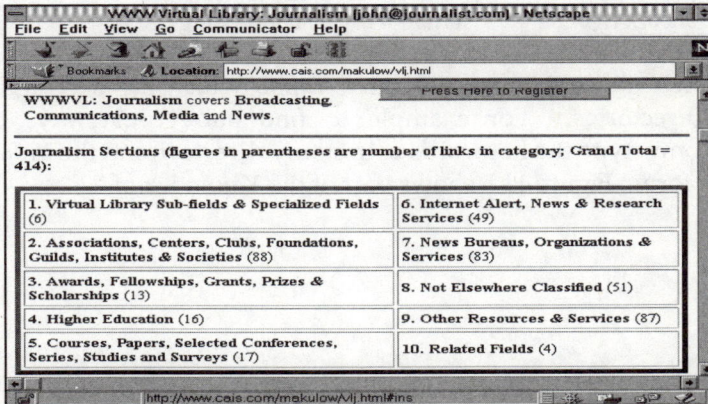

Figure 11.4 The *WWW Virtual Library* — Journalism

A listing of several directories of subject gateways is in Table 11.3 and Table 11.4 gives details of individual subject gateways.

Table 11.3 Selected list of gateway directories

Gateway directory	URL
Argus Clearinghouse	http://www.clearinghouse.net
BUBL	http://bubl.ac.uk
AlphaSearch	http://www.calvin.edu/library/as/
C&RL NewsNet Internet Resources	http://www.ala.org/acrl/resrces.html
WWW Virtual Library	http://www.vlib.edu

Table 11.4 Selected list of subject gateways

Subject Gateway	URL
ImageBase	http://www.thinker.org/index.shtml
Liszt (newsgroups)	http://www.liszt.com
Medical Matrix	http://www.medmatrix.org
OMNI (medicine)	http://www.omni.ac.uk/
Resources for Geographers	http://www.utexas.edu/depts/grg/virtdept/resources/contents.htm
Schoolwork Ugh!	http://www.schoolwork.org/

To search for subject gateways try *Yahoo* which has a category **web directories**. For example to find subject gateways on astronomy, type the keywords **astronomy directories** in the *Yahoo* search form. Figure 11.5 shows part of the *Yahoo* list of 22.

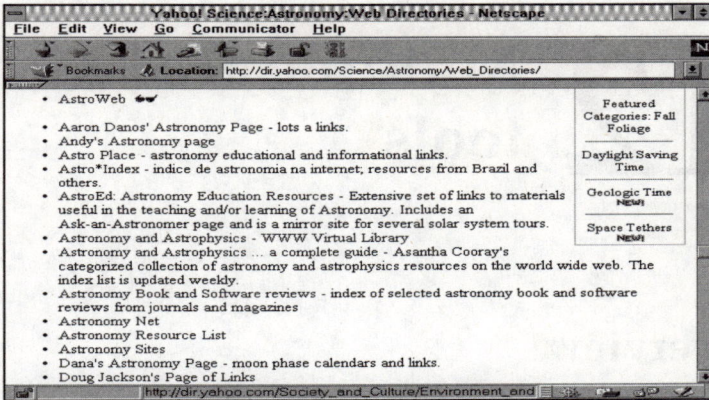

Figure 11.5 **Yahoo**'s list of Web directories of **astronomy** (2 October 1998)

Search tools by subject exercises

1. Who is responsible for the Virtual Library — Philosophy subject gateway? What is his telephone number?

2. Find a subject gateway for gardening in Canada.

3. Find an authoritative subject gateway for zoology. What rating has it been given and by whom?

12 Multiple access tools

Overview

As the number of indexes to Internet resources grows, these indexes themselves become resources that must be indexed. There are now multiple access services that provide a wide range of indexes to the subject directories, search engines and other indexes to databases such as *Medline*, *NASA Technical Reports*, and *Sport Search* (results of all Olympic Games since 1896).

The advantage of these multiple access tools is that they provide a single interface or access point to Internet indexes. There are two types of multiple access tools:

1. **Multiple access services** from their home pages present a menu, listing a choice of search tools.

2. **Meta-indexes**, often known as multi-threaded indexes or integrated search services, provide a single search form, into which you enter a search request that is sent to several search engines at the same time.

As with other Web developments, the division between these two types has become blurred. Some of the bigger sites offer access to individual search engines as well as meta-index searching.

Multiple access services

The popularity of these services is due to the fact that so many search engines are presented as a menu. They allow easy movement from one search tool to another. You do not need to remember their URLs, nor do you have to type them into the browser, and you can take advantage of the searching features of each search engine.

There is a growing number of these services, many of which are commercial, and each provides a different range of services, for example:

- a simple alphabetical list of Web search engines;
- a categorised list of Web search engines;
- a list of search engines in one subject area;
- access to other online database indexes;
- commercial document delivery of non-free documents discovered in the search.

Table 12.1 gives details of a few of these multiple access services.

Table 12.1 Features of select multiple access services

Service	URL	Features
All-in-One	http://www.albany.net/allinone	• Approximately 120 search engines listed. • Search engines are categorised into broad areas, such as the Web, software, technical reports, general and specialised interests, and people. • Gives brief annotations about each search engine.
Beaucoup	http://www.beaucoup.com	• One of the largest directories of search tools. • Categories of search tools are general and specific. • Includes an *All-On-One* page search form for general search engines.
C I Net search.com (Express Search)	http://www.search.com	• *Express Search* using 7 of the major search engines and subject directories, *Yahoo* preferred. • Access to approximately 500 databases — the *A-Z List*. • Personal subject searches. • Includes its own search engine powered by *InfoSeek*.
Directory Guide	http://www.directoryguide.com/	• Primarily for Web marketers — search tools must accept Web site announcements. • Includes a search engine.

(cont. next page)

Table 12.1 Features of select multiple access services

Service	URL	Features
Internet Sleuth	http://www.isleuth.com	• 17 of the most popular search engines and subject directories. • Quick search in broad categories such as arts, business, education, health, recreation. • 2,000 specialised databases in a hierarchical subject classification. • Sophisticated searching at any level of the subject hierarchy, including a specific source; for example **health** — **medicine** — *Journal of the American Medical Association.*
Webtaxi	http://www.webtaxi.com	• 12 of the most popular search engines and subject directories. • 'Easysearch' in broad categories such as arts, literature, business, health, and by specific source, for example *The Complete Works of Shakespeare.* • Access to *Supersearch* (a meta-index) for searching across indexes.
US Legal Research	http://gsulaw.gsu.edu/metaindex	• US legislation. • Other legal resources.

Figures 12.1–12.4 show a variety of multiple access services and some of their special features.

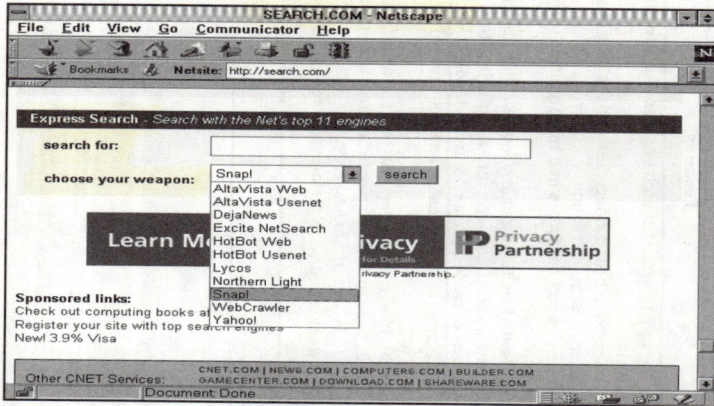

Figure 12.1 The home page of *C|Net search.com*

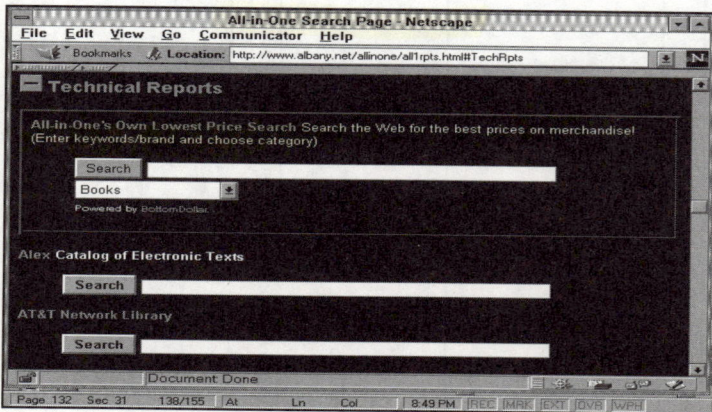

Figure 12.2 Access to indexes of a specific document type (*All-in-One*)

Internet Sleuth provides not only Web resources, but access to a vast number of non-Web online databases (its home page says 1,800). Figures 12.3 and 12.4 illustrate a search within the category **Health — Medicine** and a search of the index of a specific journal.

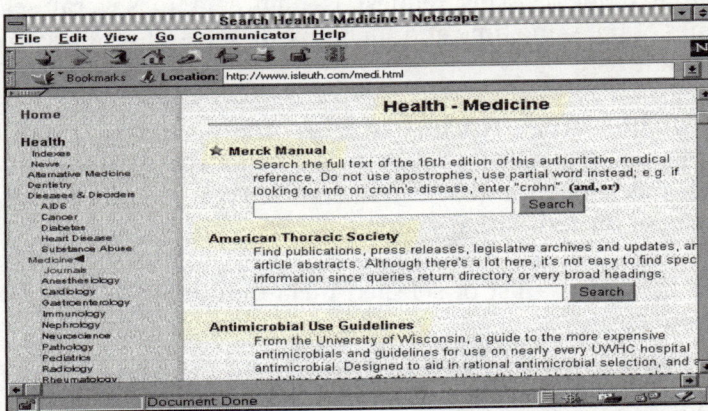

Figure 12.3 **Internet Sleuth** search in the category **Health — Medicine**

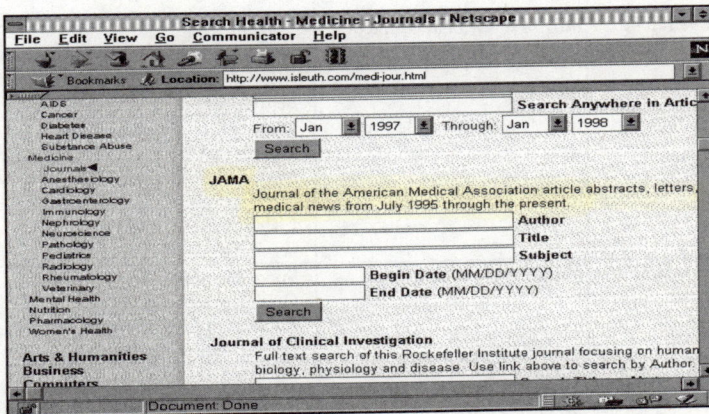

Figure 12.4 **Internet Sleuth** search in a specific journal

Meta-indexes

Meta-indexes provide a single search form into which you enter a search request. This request is then sent to several search engines at the same time and the individual results are presented as a single list.

This type of service is valuable when you need a high recall of documents on a specific subject. The major disadvantage of the search mechanism is that it does not let you use the searching features of the individual search engines.

Table 12.2 gives a list of selected meta-indexes with their URLs and some features.

Table 12.2 Selected meta-indexes

Meta-index	URL	Features
Beaucoup	http://www.beaucoup.com	• The 'Big Page'. • Single search engines. • Multiple (meta-indexes). • Search engine by categories.
Dogpile	http://www.dogpile.com	• Web, UseNet, Ftp sites, News wires. • All the major search engines, plus business news sources and news wires. • Lists results from each tool separately.
Inference Find	http://www.infind.com	• Six of the major search tools. • Groups results by subject. • Boolean queries allowed, but not all search engines use them.

(cont. next page)

Table 12.2 Selected meta-indexes

Meta-index	URL	Features
LawCrawler	http://www.lawcrawler.com	• Uses the *AltaVista* search engine. • US federal and state legal indexes. • Geographic regions. • Individual countries.
MetaCrawler	http://www.metacrawler.com	• Searches all the major search tools. • Collates the results. • Searches the Web and/or newsgroups.
SavvySearch	http://www.savvysearch.com	• Searches approximately 28 search engines, subject and people directories.
Webtaxi 'Supersearch'	http://www.webtaxi.com	• Searches up to 8 indexes at a time. Its menu includes the most popular search tools. • Indexes are divided into types, e.g. subject directories, search engines, people directories.

Figures 12.5–12.7 show how *SavvySearch* and *WebCrawler* conduct a search for the phrase 'fossil paleontology' (American spelling, not British).

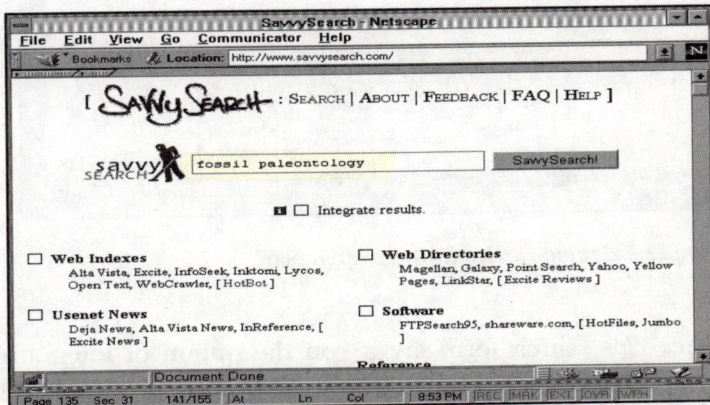

Figure 12.5 SavvySearch search form

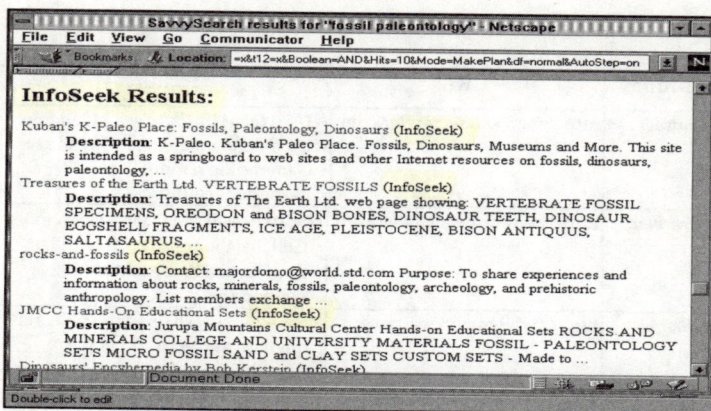

Figure 12.6 **SavvySearch** results from *InfoSeek* (October 1998)

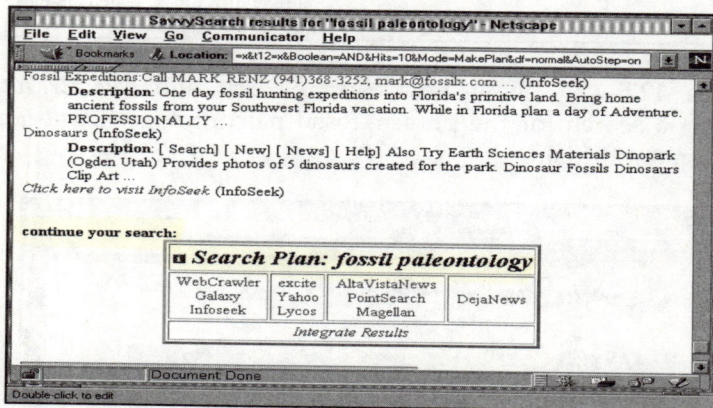

Figure 12.7 **SavvySearch**'s further search plan

SavvySearch's search form gives you the option of integrating the results or displaying the results from each search engine sequentially (Figure 12.5). It produces a chart, **Search Plan** that gives you the option to integrate the results if you have not done so, and lists on the left the search engines that produce the most results. This shows you which engine may produce more relevant results if you access it directly, using its advanced searching techniques.

MetaCrawler conducts the search across the major search engines, but instead of displaying sequentially the results from each search engine, it automatically collates them and displays them in one list.

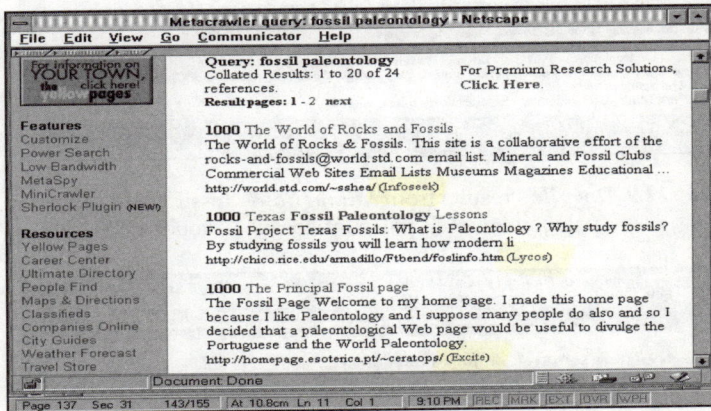

Figure 12.8 ***MetaCrawler*** collated results for 'fossil paleontology'

Notice that the index source of the site is listed at the end of the URL, for example *Lycos* in the first result in Figure 12.8.

Dogpile conducts the search across approximately 25 search tools and displays sequentially the results from each search engine. It cleverly attempts to adapt your search syntax to that of the various search tools. The search statement **fossil AND (paleontology OR palaeontology)** is sent unchanged to the *MiningCo* search engine, since it allows both Boolean and nested logic. *InfoSeek* does not accept either except by pull-down menus; therefore the query sent is **+fossil +(paleontology palaeontology)**. See Figures 12.9 and 12.10.

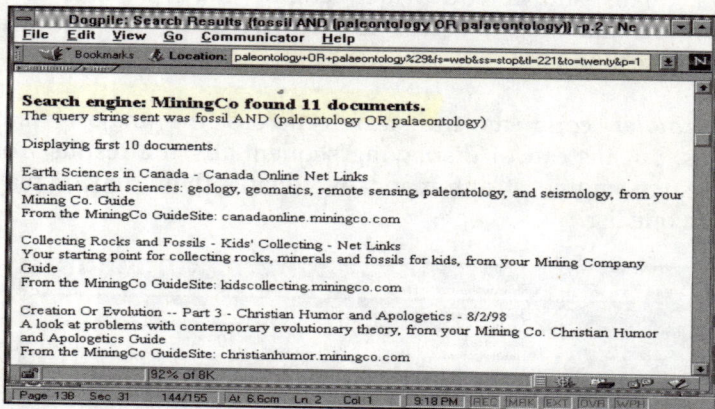

Figure 12.9 **Dogpile**'s results from **MiningCo** — 'fossil AND (paleontology OR palaeontology)' (October 1998)

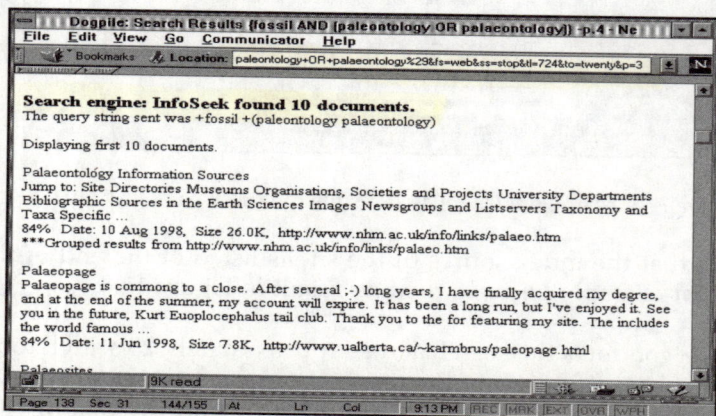

Figure 12.10 **Dogpile**'s results from **InfoSeek** — 'fossil AND (paleontology OR palaeontology)' (October 1998)

Multiple access tools exercises

1. From *Internet Sleuth* select *Excite* and search for information on tomatoes that have been genetically engineered — choose to search for only 10 seconds. Are the results different if you choose a search time of one minute?

2. Use a multiple access tool to find two New Zealand search engines.

3. Use *Dogpile* to find documents on travel in the Cook Islands. How many documents from *AltaVista* do you find? Do the same search by directly accessing *AltaVista*. Are the results the same? Are the results better if you use the proximity operator **NEAR** in the advanced *AltaVista* search?

4. Use *MetaCrawler* to find documents on 'New Zealand natural history'. Run the same search using *SavvySearch* and integrate the results. Compare the lists. Go to one of the search engines with the best results and do the search again using the advanced techniques. How many more results do you get?

5. From the **US Legal Research** meta-index, choose *Other Legal Sources*, then *LawCrawler*. Search for documents on the Australian mining industry and native title.

6. *Infomine* is a gateway to scholarly Internet resources and is one of the general Internet search tools listed on *All-in-One*. Using *Infomine* look for government information on **renewable energy**. Notice that you are given a list of related subjects.

7. You need information on 'agricultural waste management'. From *iSleuth*, select *AltaVista*. How many documents do you get? Now use *iSleuth*'s agriculture category to find non-Internet databases that may have information on this subject.

13 Effective search strategies

So how do *you* find the information you need?

Here is a simple set of guidelines that will help you to decide on a strategy to use — and to help you decide which of the many search tools to use. Remember, the more you know about you topic, the easier it is to find further information!

1. **Analyse your topic:**
   - Write down keywords, construct meaningful phrases.

2. **If you know who has the information:**
   - Go directly to their homepage.
   - Use their search engine, if there is one.

3. **To get a general idea of where to start:**
   - Use a meta-index.
   - Limit your query to two or three keywords.
   - You will get an overview of 'what's out there'.

4. **If you want general information:**
   - Use a general subject directory.
   - Use the directory's search engine — it's more effective than browsing through the hierarchies.

5. **If you are looking for a specific piece of information:**
   - Use a general search engine.
   - Use advanced searching syntax.
   - Ask for the most important keyword to be in the title.
   - Use features such as 'More like this' (*Excite*), 'Search within results' (*InfoSeek*) or 'Results ranking' (*AltaVista*).

6. **If you want general information in a specific area or topic:**
   - Use a subject gateway.
   - Give preference to authoritative subject gateways.

7. **If you want a specific piece of information in a specific area or topic:**
   - Use a specialised search engine.
   - Use advanced searching syntax, if available.
   - Ask for the most important keyword of phrase to be in the title, if the syntax is allowed.

14 Developments

The Internet is continuing to grow at an enormous pace, and search tools are constantly changing in an attempt to keep up with this growth. Anyone who is serious about information searching needs to monitor the Internet constantly for new technologies and tools as they become available. This chapter looks at some of the developments that are making an impact on the effectiveness of the Internet as an information resource.

Site search engines

The first edition of this book, in the chapter on *New developments*, examined the *Harvest* system, one of the earlier software programs that allowed an individual Web site to be indexed and therefore to be searched. Since then many large Web sites have installed server search engines. Most of the popular general Internet search engines can be found on individual sites; indeed server search software is a very competitive industry. Table 14.1, page 144, gives a selection of the software available for indexing Web sites.

Why is it helpful to index individual Web sites?

The most effective strategy for finding information is to go to the site you know has the information. As an individual site is focussed on a particular area or topic, a site search engine allows information to be found quickly and directly. It's like finding the right book and consulting its index!

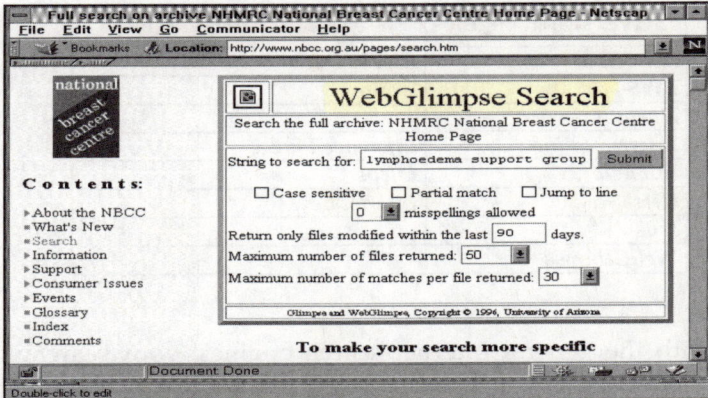

Figure 14.1 Example of a server search engine (*WebGlimpse*)

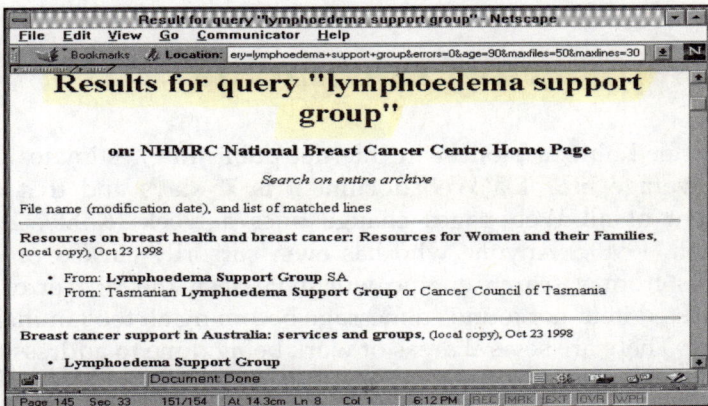

Figure 14.2 Example of a **site** query result

Table 14.1 is a list of some of the Web server search engines you will find at Web sites; some of them are also general Internet search engines.

Table 14.1 List of selected Web server search engines

Server search engine	Internet search engine
AltaVista	*AltaVista*
EWS	*Excite*
Harvest	
Inference Find	*Inference Find*
Inmagic	*Lycos*
UltraSeek	*InfoSeek*
Isys	
WebGlimpse	

As with the general Internet search engines, your searching is more effective if you use the advanced features. If the server search engine is not one you are familiar with, READ THE **HELP** DOCUMENTATION.

'Disappearing' documents

Brewster Kahle, a pioneer in Internet publishing, estimates that the average life of a Web document is 75 days and that one percent of all Web pages change once a week (Kahle, 1997; Lyman, 1998). Anyone who has even cursorily clicked on the results from a search engine will have seen the '404 error — requested item not found', a message becoming all too familiar to users. There are several areas of work being done to address this problem.

URNs and PURLs

An URN (Uniform Resource Name) is the name that identifies a resource or unit of information independent of its location (URL). URNs are globally unique, persistent and accessible over the network. The work being done on this naming scheme is headed up by Internet Engineering Task Force (IETF). *D-Lib Magazine*, February 1996, contains a very good explanatory article on URNs <http://www.dlib.org/dlib/february96/02arms.html>.

PURLs (Persistent Uniform Resource Locators) are a result of the work being done by OCLC in the URN standards and with the library cataloguing committees. Very simply, a PURL is an URL with an extra bit called a *resolver address*. Thus, instead of pointing directly to the location of an Internet resource, the PURL points to an intermediate redirection service. PURLs are considered to be an intermediate step toward the future when URNs will be an integral part of the Internet architecture.

Internet Archive Project

There is much concern in library, archives and museum circles and in the mind of Brewster Kahle that much of the world's cultural heritage as represented by documents on the Internet is not being saved for future generations. The result of this concern is *Alexa*, a software program, and the *Internet Archive* project.

Alexa is a spider that began to crawl the Web in mid-1996, downloading entire sites, thus collecting 'snapshots' of the Web. The company, *Alexa Internet* <http://www.alexa.com>, donates these downloaded documents to the *Internet Archive*. At the time of writing the Archive contains 8 terabytes of documents and

in October 1998 two terabytes, about 500,000 pages, were donated
to the Library of Congress.

For searchers on the Internet there is the side benefit from the
Internet Archive. Download and install the *Alexa* client software
on your computer and whenever you get the '404 error' click on
Alexa's 'Archive' button and it will retrieve for you a copy of the
'disappeared' document if it is in the *Internet Archive*.

Figure 14.3 shows the *Netscape* browser with the *Alexa* toolbar
at the bottom. The **Archive** button is on the right.

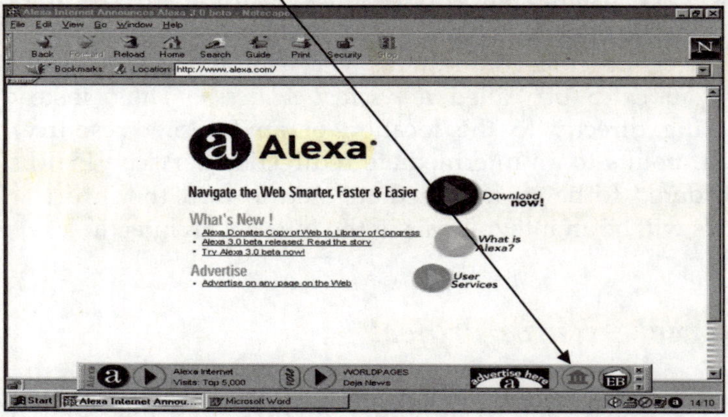

Figure 14.3 The *Alexa* toolbar at the bottom of the browser

Another service of *Alexa* is discussed in Chapter 16 *Evaluating
information*.

Individual site searching exercises

1. Go to the home page of the University of New South Wales <http://unsw.edu.au>. Can you find a policy document about the library's collection development?

2. Find information about the fees for residential care for the aged from the Australian Commonwealth Department of Health and Family Services <http://www.health.gov.au>

3. From the Australian Department of Immigration and Multicultural Affairs <http://www.immi.gov.au> find a copy of the 1998 Review of the point system.

15 Organising your information

Overview

The information on the Internet tends to fall into two general categories:

1. 'Real' documents.
2. Sites.

In the context of this book, a 'real' document is the data you are looking for, for example a stockmarket report, a journal article or a policy document. A 'site' is a home page that points to another resource — for example, home pages of organisations or of services such as subject directories, search engines and library catalogues.

Every document and site has an address, a URL. While we often print or save to file 'real' documents, in most cases we simply need to know how to access the information — in other words, how to gain access to a list of the URLs. This can be done by creating bookmarks as you access various sites. Since it is very easy to accumulate dozens of bookmarks, it becomes important to organise them so that you can quickly find the one you want. In practice, what you need is your own personal subject directory to the Web, which you can create by using bookmarks.

Bookmarks

You should classify your bookmarks so that you can retrieve the information immediately. If you use the same subject headings or categories that you use in your information centre, you will be able to incorporate the information easily into the catalogue or database.

If you are accumulating bookmarks for your personal files, you should develop a list of subject categories that reflect your interests and area of research. This list of subject categories should be structured into broad categories that can be sub-divided. (See *Subject classification and thesauruses* section, page 42.) Table 15.1 gives a simple example.

Table 15.1 Sample subject categories

Government information
  Use for official government home pages
    Australia
    New Zealand
    Papua New Guinea
    United Kingdom
Libraries
    Australia
      Academic
      Corporate
      Public & Government
    New Zealand
    United States

Creating folders

Netscape allows you to organise your bookmarks into subject categories by setting up **folders** into which you place the appropriate bookmarks. Using the example given in Table 15.1, Figures 15.1–15.5 show how to set up folders for the first level category **Government information**.

Select **Bookmarks** from the toolbar, then the option **Edit Bookmarks**.

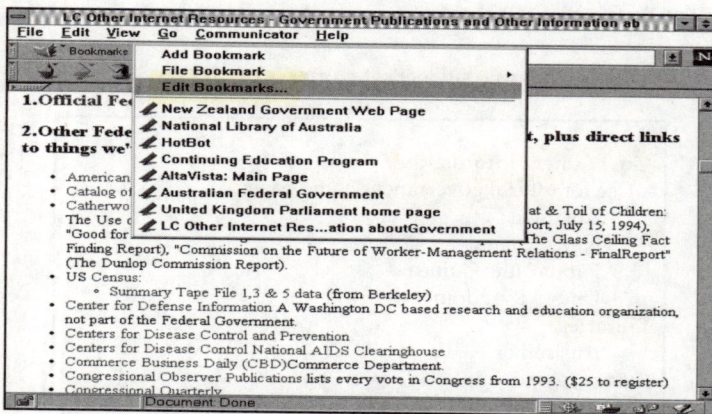

Figure 15.1 **Netscape Bookmarks** menu

This brings up the **Bookmarks** application that runs in *Netscape*, but separately from the browser, and shows your bookmarks as a file (bookmark.htm).

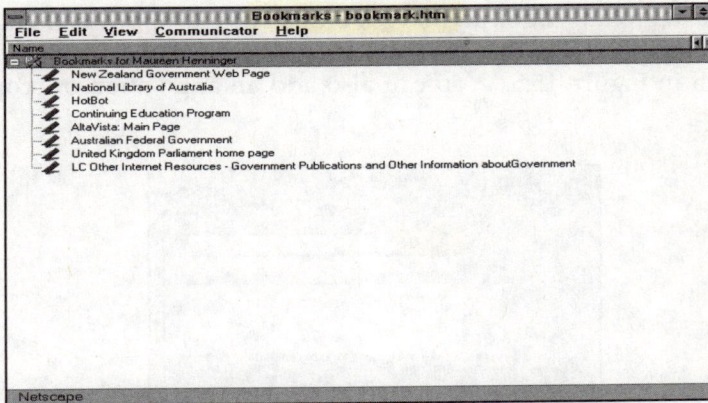

Figure 15.2 List of bookmarks as a file (bookmark.htm)

The new folder **Government information** is a first level category of bookmarks, for example, 'Bookmarks for Maureen Henninger' (see Figure 15.2). You should make sure that you have this item highlighted (click on it to do so). To insert a folder, select **File** then **New Folder**.

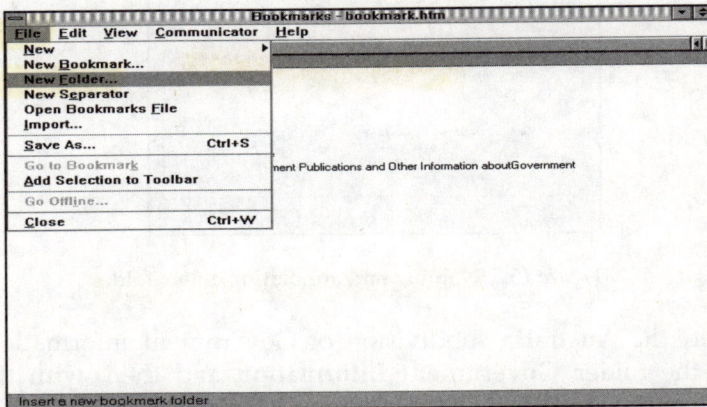

Figure 15.3 Inserting a new folder

In the template, **Bookmark Properties**, which appears (Figure 15.4), simply type the subject category over **New Folder**, as shown in Figure 15.5. You can also add an annotation or scope note.

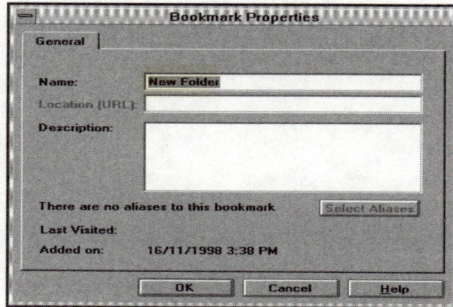

Figure 15.4 New folder template

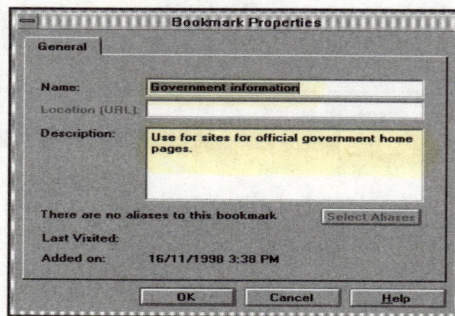

Figure 15.5 Naming and annotating a new folder

To add the **Australia** subdivision of Government information, open the folder **Government information** and then, with the procedure just outlined, insert a new folder for Australia.

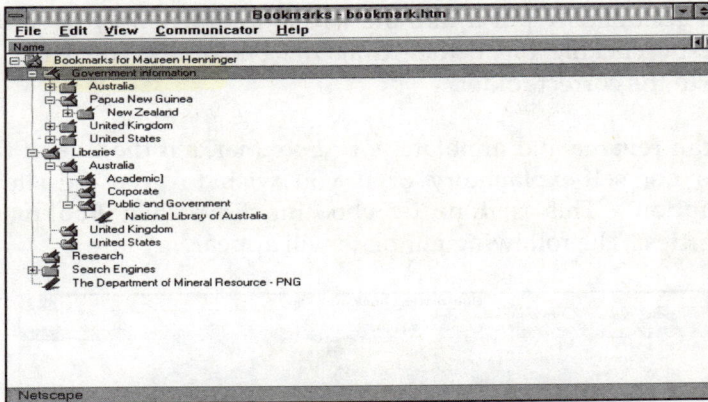

Figure 15.6 Hierarchical bookmark folders

New bookmarks are added to the bottom of your bookmark list. *Netscape* allows you to rearrange your bookmarks with a 'drop and drag' facility. Point to the new bookmark and, holding the mouse button down, drag the bookmark up and drop it onto the appropriate folder by letting go of the mouse button.

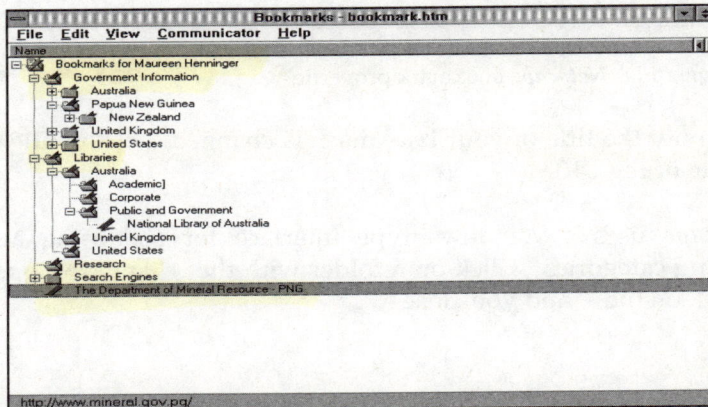

Figure 15.7 New bookmark appended to the bookmark list

If you accidentally put it into the wrong folder, simply open the folder by clicking on it, then drag the bookmark you want to move to the correct folder.

You can rename and annotate your bookmarks if the title of the site is not self-explanatory or if you wish to give the site a description. This is done by choosing **Edit**, then **Bookmark Properties**. The following template will appear.

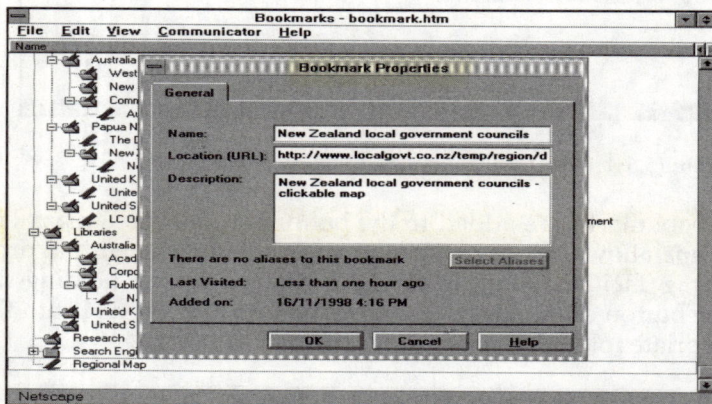

Figure 15.8 **Netscape** bookmark properties

Note: only the title of your bookmark is changed, not the title of the site or the URL.

Netscape uses a Windows type interface for collapsing and opening categories. Click on a folder with the '+' and you open it; click on the '-' and you close it.

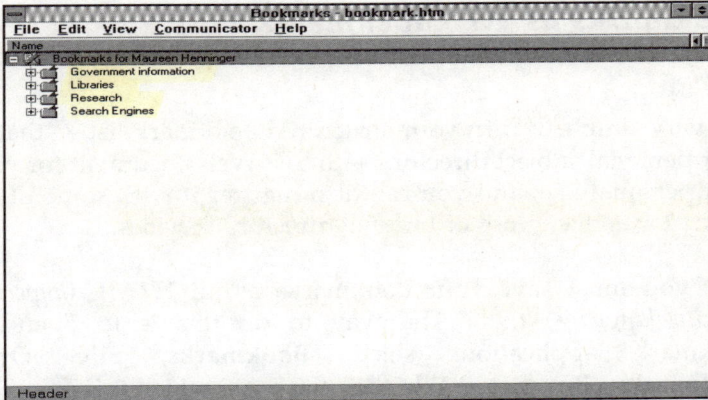

Figure 15.9 Closed *Netscape* folders

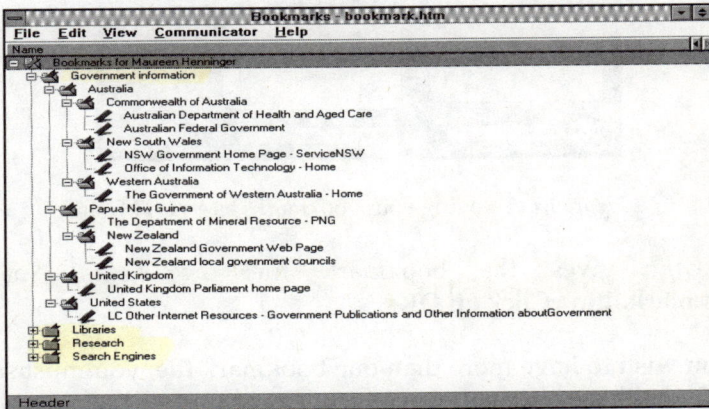

Figure 15.10 Opened *Netscape* folders

Bookmarks as Web documents

It is very simple to turn your structured bookmark list — that is, your personal subject directory — into a Web document for your own personal use, and you can also register it with some of the Internet search engines or Internet directory services.

First you must save your bookmarks as an **HTML** (*hypertext markup language*) file. The way to do this is to open the bookmark application (select **Bookmarks**, **File**, **Open Bookmarks File**). Select **File** then **Save As**, which brings up the following template.

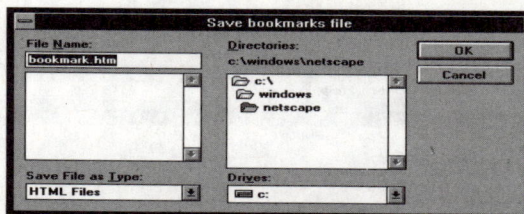

Figure 15.11 Saving your bookmarks as an **HTML** file

Netscape gives the bookmark file the default name **bookmark.htm**. Click on **OK**.

If you wish to have more than one bookmark file, you must save the file with another name. (Assuming, of course, that you wish to edit your bookmark list for different purposes, for example to create a series of subject directories.)

To open this as a Web document, from *Netscape,* select **File**, then **Open Page**, type in the name of your file and click on **Open** (this is opening a local document). If you cannot remember the name of your file, click on **Choose File,** find the right directory and select **bookmark.htm** and click on **OK.**

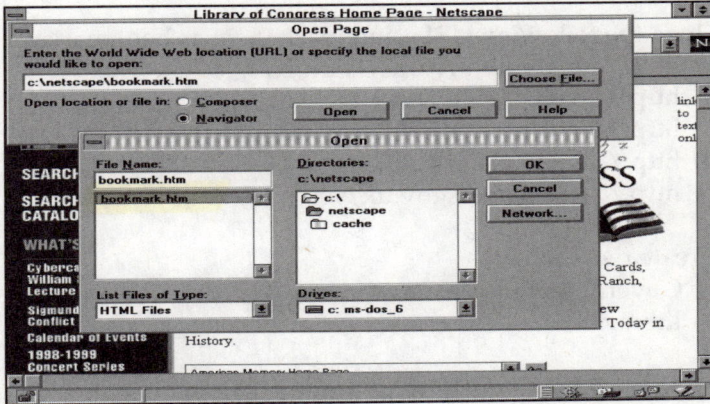

Figure 15.12 Opening a bookmark file as a Web document

This is how your bookmark file will look as a Web document.

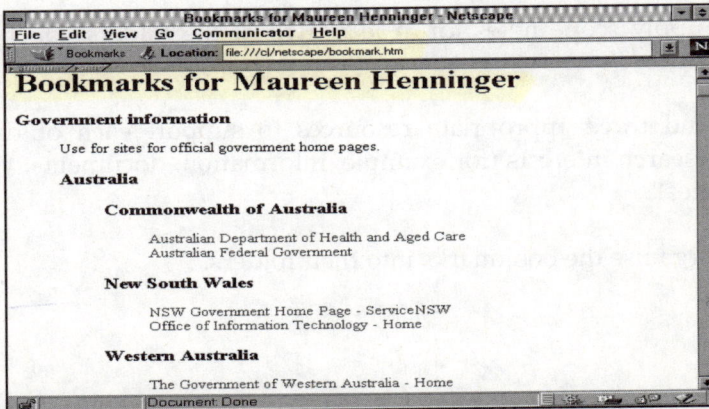

Figure 15.13 Your bookmark file as a Web document

Bookmarks exercises

1. Open the following URLs and mark them as bookmarks:
    a) http://www.library.unsw.edu.au
    b) http://www.fish.govt.nz
    c) http://www.loc.gov (Library of Congress, US)
    d) http://www.nla.gov.au/
    e) http://www.open.gov.uk/

2. Create two folders:
    a) Government information
    b) Libraries

3. Place the bookmarks into the appropriate folders.

4. Choose two subject areas you are interested in, subdivide each into sub-categories by allocating narrower terms, and create the appropriate folders.

5. Supply scope notes for at least two of the folders you have created.

6. Find three appropriate resources to support each of these research interests (for example, information, documents, Web sites).

7. Organise the bookmarks into their folders.

16 Evaluating information

Criteria

You should be as particular about the quality of Internet information as you are about 'traditional' information. Alastair Smith (Smith, 1997) lists about 25 criteria for evaluating Internet information resources. The major ones are the source, date, content and authenticity of the document or site.

Source

Anyone can publish anything on the Internet, therefore the task of finding material that is authoritative is imperative. Here are some pointers:

- Can you identify the author or producer and his/her organisation?
- What are the author's credentials and expertise?
- What is the authority and reputation of the author's sponsor, publisher or organisation?
- Is there any contact information for the author or organisation?
- A URL with a tilde '~' is generally a personal, not official URL.

Figures 16.1 and 16.2 show two Web documents whose author details (Auer, 1998 and Lahita, 1996) are very well documented.

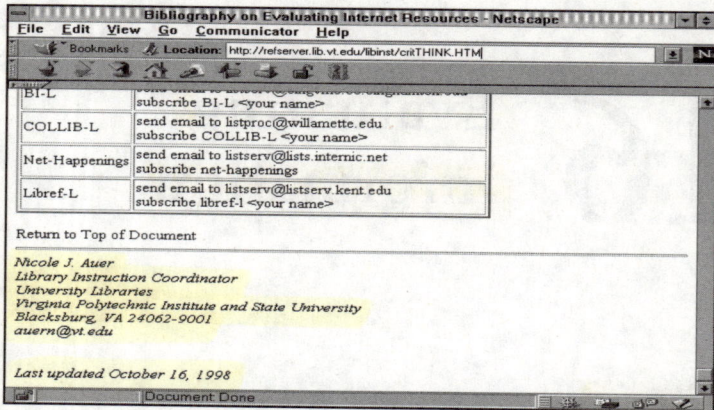

Figure 16.1 Document footer showing source and publication information

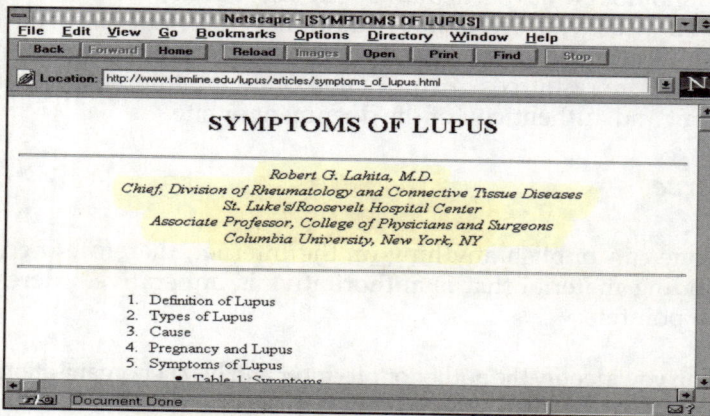

Figure 16.2 Document giving details of the author's credentials

Date

The Internet is a dynamic environment that in theory enables the publication of up-to-date information. Unfortunately it is often difficult to ascertain when the material was created, and if it has been changed subsequently. The points you should look for concerning the date of publication are:

- When was the document or Web page first produced?
- Is there any date of revision?
- Is there evidence that the author or producer regularly maintains the links in the document?

The example in Figure 16.2 also contains 'Date last modified 1996-07-30' at the bottom of the document (Lahita, 1996).

Content

We have already looked at the authority and accuracy of Internet sources, however there are other determinants of content quality.

- Does the material match the needs of the target audience?
- Is it suitable for your needs?
- Is the document/site well structured and information well presented so that it is easy to navigate?
- If there are graphics, do they complement the information or do they detract from it?
- Is the site easily accessible and stable? Is the site's computer often 'down' or does a document from there take 'forever' to load?

A very helpful tool for evaluating information is *Alexa* (see Chapter 14, pages 145-46, for a full discussion about this tool).

As *Alexa* takes its 'snapshots' of the Web it gathers very useful statistics about the sites, such as data about the site registration and the 'freshness' of the site. To get this site metadata simply click on **arrow** icon on the *Alexa* toolbar as shown in Figure 16.3.

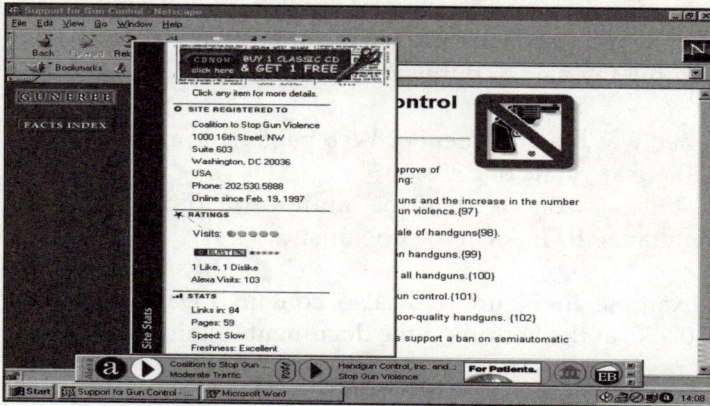

Figure 16.3 Metadata about a Web site gathered by *Alexa*

Authenticity

Can you tell if a document has been 'tampered with' or changed? This is difficult, however the are two technologies, *digital signatures* and *digital watermarks*, that may be used to help ensure the authenticity of documents. At the time of writing these technologies are not generally used for Web documents.

A digital signature is a logical *hash* (mathematical summary) of information coded using a key unique to the signer. It has properties that can help one accurately identify the creator of the hash and determine whether the original information or hash was tampered with.

Digital watermarks can be visible or invisible. Figure 16.4 shows a visible watermark on a document, thus proclaiming the ownership of the information. Watermarks generally are designed to be robust (that is, cannot be destroyed). However one type of invisible watermark, the *fragile* watermark, which requires an authentication key, *is* destroyed by any attempt to alter the material.

Figure 16.4 Digital watermark on scanned manuscript from the Vatican Library <http://www.software.hosting.ibm.com/is/dig-lib/vatican/ manuscript.html>

For further information about digital watermarks, see Fred Mintzer's article 'Safeguarding digital library contents and users' in *D-Lib Magazine*, December 1997.

Metadata standards

The development of metatdata standards for Web documents could be very helpful in ascertaining some of this criteria. For example, the *Dublin Core* metadata standards recommend that information concerning authorship and date be included in the document's metadata (see Figure 16.5):

```
<META NAME="DC.Creator.PersonalName"
CONTENT="Henninger, Maureen">
<META NAME="DC.Creator.PersonalName.Address"
CONTENT="m.henninger@unsw.edu.au">
<META NAME="DC.Publisher" CONTENT="School of
Information, Library and Archive Studies, University of New South
Wales"
```

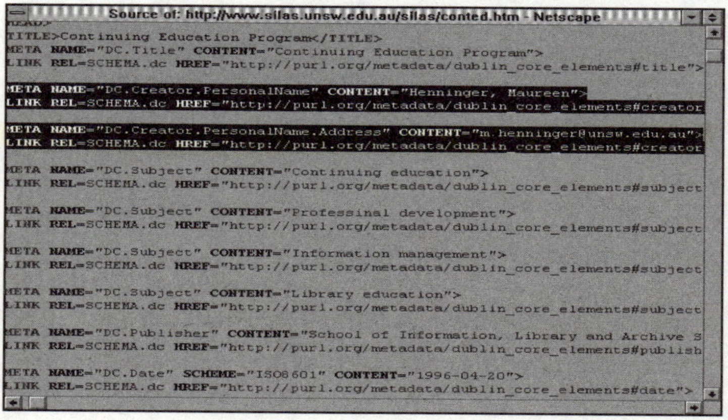

Figure 16.5 Document source showing *Dublin Core* metadata standards

Although a lot of work is being done on metadata standards, in reality few Web documents contain authorship and date metadata.

17 Copyright and citations

Copyright

There are no uniform or well-defined laws yet for electronic media, which of course includes information on the Internet. However, according to the *Report of the Working Group on Intellectual Property Rights* (the group is part of the US Government's Information Infrastructure Task Force), displaying an image or file on the Internet is equivalent to displaying it on television, in an art gallery or in print — only the copyright owner has this privilege. Transmitting an image or file on the Internet is equivalent to reproducing and distributing that image; the rights to reproduce and distribute belong exclusively to the copyright owner.

The WIPO (World Intellectual Property Organisation) Database Treaty of 1996 made the following statements and recommendations concerning electronic (Internet) sources:

- Rejection of the proposal to include all temporary electronic copies, that is browsing online, within the scope of the reproduction right.
- A broad right of communication to the public be given to the rightsholders.

- The limitation and exceptions (fair dealing, fair use, education and library exceptions) permitted under the Berne Convention remain largely intact.
- The contracting parties are obliged to protect copyright holders against the circumvention of technological copyright protection measures, for example decoders (Australian Government Solicitor, 1997).

Digital watermarks and digital signatures as techniques for providing authenticity have already been described in the previous chapter, pages 162-63. However it has been pointed out that 'one major application for digital watermarking is to convey *ownership* information...and may identify the originator of the material, or it may identify the recipient (the end-user of library) to whom the material was given'. In the case of using watermarks to identify the recipient, persons who post copyrighted material on the Web risk exposing their identities (Mintzer et al, 1997).

Therefore it is best to observe the following print copyright laws when dealing with electronic media:

1. Assume that all information on the Web is in some way copyrighted; *never* assume that it is public property.
2. If you copy any material from the Web, give proper credit to the author.
3. If you put your own material on the Internet, add a copyright notice.

Citing Internet sources

The standard format for citing Web sources is to use the URL. The appendix to RFC1738 (Request for Comments: 1738, an Internet standard) suggests that it be placed inside <>, for example:

<http://clever.net/quinion/words/articles/citation.htm>

Quinion (1996) suggests the best way to handle the dating of the document: '...if the accessed document is dated internally, use that date for the citation. If there is no date given, use the date at which it was first accessed (prefixed by "Accessed" in parentheses, as shown below). Optionally, give both (for example, if you have any reason to think the document may have been amended since its nominal date of creation).' A reference to his document would be:

Quinion, Michael B. (1996). *Citing online sources: Advice on online citation formats.*
<http://clever.net/quinion/words/articles/citation.htm>, (updated 11 Feb 1998, accessed 10 Oct 1998).

Epilogue

Now that you are familiar with the Web and are armed with some sensible techniques for retrieving the information you need (although 'surfing' is still a great deal of fun), here are a few final pointers.

The Internet itself is the best resource for learning about the Internet. The Bibliography and References included indicate the variety and wealth of information available to you, and I would recommend that you browse through these sources.

The Internet is mainly used for communication and much of its valuable information is communicated by the discussion groups, such as Listservs. Become an active participant in these discussions to keep up with developments and to find which sites others have found useful.

Use the printed media too to keep up — for example, *The Australian* newspaper's *Syte* supplement every Saturday.

Finally, become proficient and exploit the potential riches. Above all, **enjoy the experience**.

Answers to exercises

URL construction exercises (page 17)

1. *Sausage* Company   http://www.sausage.com.au

2. Northern Territory
   Government   http://www.nt.gov.au

3. National Library of
   Australia   http://www.nla.gov.au

4. New Zealand Customs   http://www.customs.govt.nz

5. Harvard University   http://www.harvard.edu

6. The Australian Archives   http://www.aa.gov.au

7. The NSW Department
   of Health   http://www.health.nsw.gov.au

8. Cambridge University   http://www.cam.ac.uk

9. Curtis Davis Garrard   http://www.cdg.co.uk

10. Smithsonian Institution   http://www.si.edu

People directories exercises (page 72)

1. m.henninger@unsw.edu.au — found on *Four11*, *WhoWhere*, *IAF*, and the University of New South Wales home page directory services.

2. There are four. Use *Telstra's Yellowpages* and request newsagents as the type of business, Bendigo as the town and Victoria as the state.

3. vice-chancellor@vcc.usyd.edu.au — construct the URL for the University of Sydney's home page (http://www.usyd.edu.au), and follow the links **general information**, **vice-chancellor's welcome**, and **contact numbers**.

4. NASMPAO@SIVM.SI.EDU — use the home page of the Smithsonian Institution (http://www.si.edu). Select the **On-line Telephone Directory**, then **Departmental Directory Information**; the department is the National Air and space Museum.

5. (602) 813-8012 — construct the homepage URL (http://www.polydrive.com) or use *IAF* (Internet Address Finder).

6. Yes, Ross Todd is affiliated with the University — the URL is **www.uts.edu.au** and follow the links **information & resources** and **phone directory**.

Subject directories exercises (page 91)

1. *Galaxy*'s categories and sub-categories are all on the one page.

2. No 'right' answer. This exercise is to let you become familar with the features and content of some of the subject directories.

3. *LookSmart*: Society & Politics — Politics — Campaigns & Elections — Elections Int'l
Snap: People & Society: Politics: Elections: International Elections. Listings are very different.

4. No right answer. See 2 above.

5. Dr T. Matthew Ciolek.

Search engine exercises (page 119)

1. Search for the word **ecotourism**, selecting the date after January 1998. Modify the results to should contain the phrase **New South Wales** and should contain the word **NSW.**

Specifying **Oceania** reduces the number (all documents retrieved must have a country domain somewhere in Oceania). By choosing **.au** the search is narrowed down further.

2. Here are two possibilities using *AltaVista* which allows ranging by date:
title:diabetes AND "the elderly"
"elderly diabet*"

3. *WebCrawler*: a possible search statement:
   "global warming" AND "health effects" AND (Australia OR Oceania).
However, leaving out **effects**, would produce many more documents.

AltaVista: search statement:
"global warming" and "health effects" and (Australia or Oceania) and request ranking on **global** and **health**. This will produce about ten times as many documents.

4. *NorthernLight*: about 180. Search query **title:"search engines" AND title:research**
AltaVista about 110. Same search query. The results are different from those of *NorthernLight*.

5. *AltaVista*: **control* NEAR advert*** and 'user rank' **Luria**.

6. *AltaVista* (as you can search by language and it has a translation service). Search query **disappeared NEAR Argentina** and choose Spanish from the language menu. Click on 'translate' to get the document in English.

Search tools by subject exercises (page 127)

1. *Virtual Library* <http://www.vlib.org>. Dan Brickley. Tel. no. is 928 7493 — click on University of Bristol at bottom of homepage; look for online telephone directory.

2. *ICanGarden*. Search on *Yahoo* **gardening Canada directories**.

3. *Internet Resource Guide for Zoology*. **Argus Clearinghouse** — 5
   checks; *eBlast* (Encyclopaedia Britannica) — 2 stars.

Multiple access tools exercises (page 139)

1. Search statement: "genetically engineered" AND tomato*
   No difference in results with longer searching time.

2. Use either *Beaucoup* — geographically specific (at the time of
   writing *eDirectory* has no listings for New Zealand).
   NZ Explorer, Access New Zealand.

3. Search statement **"Cook Islands" travel**. The statement sent
   to *AltaVista* is **"Cook Islands" AND travel** — produces
   approximately 4768 documents. Searching *AltaVista* directly
   "Cook Islands" NEAR travel produces approximately 520
   dopcuments which appear far more relevant.

4. *MetaCrawler*: as a phrase 'New Zealand natural history'.
   Approximately 16.
   SavvySearch: the same search. About the same number.
   Excite: "New Zealand" AND "natural history", about 2,600.

5. Some possibilities:
   (Australia* near mining near industry) and (native near title)
   (Australia* near mining near (industr* or company or
   companies) and (native near title)

6. No 'right' answer.

7. *AltaVista* search as a phrase "agricultural waste management" — about 500 documents. From the *iSleuth* category **agriculture**, the best link is **See Also: iSleuth: U.S. Department of Agriculture**. Search statement "waste management". You should not use the term agriculture since almost all documents will have this term. Note that when you search this database, you are searching the GILS (Government Information Loactor Service) metadata respository. This is similar to the AGLS (see page 51).

Individual site searching exercise (page 147)

1. UNSW uses *UltraSeek* (*InfoSeek*). Use the advanced searching and search for 'policy' in the title, 'collection development' as a phrase, and 'library' as a keyword.

2. For highly relevant documents, search for the phrase 'residential care' in the title, 'fees' in the title, and 'aged' as a keyword.

3. This is the *Excite* server search engine which allows Boolean operators. The following search query will give you a good result: "point system" AND review AND 1998

Glossary

This is a brief glossary of terms used in this book. For more terms, see **http://whatis.com/index.htm**

AARNet Australian Academic Research Network.

address See **IP address**.

anchor A hypertext link within the same document.

application Software that performs a specific useful function, for example email application.

Archie A system for locating files that are publicly available by Anonymous FTP.

ARPANet Advanced Research Projects Agency Network.

bits per second The speed at which bits are transmitted over a communications medium.

bookmarks A link to a Web site that has been saved and added to a list of saved links (sometimes called a 'hotlist').

browser Software which allows you to access the World Wide Web.

cache A cache is a place to store something more or less temporarily. See also **cache memory** and **disk cache**.

cache memory Random access memory (RAM) that a computer microprocessor can access more quickly than it can access regular RAM.

catalogue An index or directory of information.

CERN European Laboratory for Particle Physics, in Geneva, Switzerland, where the World Wide Web was developed.

client Software application which requests a service for you from a server somewhere on the network.

CWIS Campus Wide Information Service, information and services made publicly available at universities.

disk cache A mechanism for improving the time it takes to read from or write to a hard disk. The disk cache holds data that has recently been read, such as a Web document.

DNS Domain Name System is the way that Internet domain names are located and translated into IP (Internet Protocol) addresses.

domain Organisation level used to identify users on the Internet.

domain name Locates an organisation on the Internet using an easily remembered 'handle' rather than the numbers of the IP address.

download To copy a file from another computer (the Internet) to your computer.

email Electronic mail.

FAQ Frequently Asked Questions; FAQ sheets are available on many topics.

flame A nasty, often personal attack against the author of a posting in a newsgroup.

form A page set up as a data entry form, which then acts on your request (for example, a keyword search).

FTP File Transfer Protocol (one of the TCP/IP suite of protocols); it defines how files are transferred from one computer to another.

gateway A computer system which transfers data between incompatible networks or applications.

gopher A text-based hierarchical classification of information, presented as menus; there are gopher clients and gopher servers.

hit A document (that is, an item listed in search results) that is relevant to your needs.

Home page An entry point for access to the World Wide Web.

host A computer that provides information; also called a server.

hotlist A list of saved Internet addresses or links (called 'bookmarks' on the Web).

HTML Hypertext Markup Language, used for creating Web documents.

HTTP Hypertext Transfer Protocol, the protocol used for retriev-ing Web documents.

hyperlink A hypertext link in a home page, usually denoted by a different colour from the main body of text.

Internet A global network of networks, all using the suite of communication protocols TCP/IP.

IP address Internet Protocol Address, a unique address identifying each computer on the Internet.

IRC chat A service that allows large group conversations in written form over the Internet.

LAN Local Area Network, a network of interconnected workstations sharing the resources of a single server within a relatively small geographic area, such as one floor of a building.

link Usually refers to a hypertext link in Web documents.

Listserv A small program that automatically redistributes email to names on a mailing list. The term is also used for a discussion group to which you subscribe.

Lynx A Web browser that can display only text, not graphics or sound.

metadata Data about data; data definitions describing aspects of actual data items, such as name, author, date and format.

mirror site A site that duplicates files also held at another site or sites on the Internet.

Mosaic A Web browser.

NCSA National Center for Supercomputing Applications at the University of Illinois in Urbana, Illinois.

Net Usually an abbreviation for the Internet.

Netscape A Web browser.

newsgroup A forum for discussing a variety of topics on the Internet.

OCLC Online Computer Library Center, Inc. a nonprofit, library computer service and research organisation.

packet switching A system for transferring information across a network.

PPP Point to Point Protocol; it allows a computer to use the Internet protocols (TCP/IP) with a standard telephone line and high speed modem. It is replacing SLIP connections.

protocol The special set of rules of communication that the terminals or nodes (and related software) in a telecommunication connection use when they send signals back and forth.

RFC An Internet or other technical standard or formal document that is the result of committee drafting and subsequent review by interested parties.

scalability The capacity for a computer application or product (hardware or software) to continue to function well as it (or its context) is rescaled (typically, to a larger size, but possibly to a smaller size).

search engine A program that allows you to search for specific data on the Web.

server Software that allows a computer to offer a service to another computer; it refers also to the computer on which the service runs, for example a Web server.

SLIP Serial Line IP, a protocol that allows a computer to use the Internet protocols (TCP/IP) with a standard telephone line and high-speed modem.

SMTP Simple Mail Transfer Protocol that allows email over the Internet (one of the TCP/IP suite of protocols).

SOIF Summary Object Interchange Format, for storing information in the *Harvest* system.

TCP/IP Transmission Control Protocol and Internet Protocol, for controlling Internet traffic.

Telnet Network terminal emulation protocol (one of the TCP/IP suite of protocols) allowing your computer to behave as a remote computer; also known as 'remote login'.

URL Uniform Resource Locator, the addressing system for Web documents.

UseNet A newsgroup system that is not part of the Internet, but is accessible across it.

UUCP UNIX to UNIX Copy Protocol for copying files between UNIX systems; UseNet news services were built on this system.

Veronica A service for searching gopher sites for menu items (similar to Archie which searches FTP sites).

WAIS Wide Area Information Service, a powerful system for searching the full text of databases across the Internet; many search engines use it.

WAN Wide Area Network.

Web An abbreviation for the World Wide Web.

Web browser Software (*Explorer*, *Lynx*, *Mosaic*, *Netscape*) that allows you to access the Web; also referred to as a Web client.

Web server A computer that contains Web documents and runs HTTP software.

WWW World Wide Web, the distributed hypermedia system.

Bibliography

1. Auer, Nicole J. (1998). *Bibliography on Evaluating Internet Resources*.
   <http://refserver.lib.vt.edu/libinst/critTHINK.HTM>,
   (Last updated 8 Sept 1998, accessed 6 Oct 1998).

2. Australian Government Solicitor (1997). 'Copyright — into the digital age'. *Legal Briefing No. 31*, 10 March 1997.
   <http://www.law.gov.au/publications/lpb/31copyright.htm>,
   (accessed 29 June 1998).

3. Barry, Tony and Joanna Richardson (1996). *Indexing the Net: A Review of Indexing Tools*.
   <http://bond.edu.au/Bond/Library/People/jpr/ausweb96/>,
   (last revised: 11 July 1996, accessed 10 Oct 1998).

4. Calafia, Danny (1998). *A Webmaster's Guide to Search Engines*.
   <http://searchenginewatch.com/webmasters/index.html>,
   (accessed 10 Oct 1998).

5. Carvin, Andy (1997). 'Paving the first path: The Internet' in *EdWeb: Exploring Technology and School Reform*.
   <http://sunsite.unc.edu/edweb/index.html>, (last updated 14 Sept 1998, accessed 10 Oct 1998).

6. Conners, Kathryn L. (1996). *The PartheNet: Combined Internet Resources for Students of Art History*.
   <http://www.mtholyoke.edu/~klconner/parthenet.html>,
   (last updated 1 Nov 1998, accessed 5 Nov 1998).

7. Day, Michael and Neil Beagrie (1998). *Metadata: DELOS6: Preservation of Digital Information.* <http://www.ariadne.ac.uk/issue16/delos/>, (last updated 13 July 1998, accessed 10 Oct 1998)

8. Eagan, Ann and L. Bender (1996). 'Spiders and worms and crawlers, oh my: searching on the World Wide Web'. *Untangling the Web.* Proceedings of the Conference, 26 April 1996. University of California, Santa Barbara. <http://www.library.ucsb.edu/untangle/eagan.html>, (accessed 18 July 1996).

9. Grassian, Esther (1997). *Thinking Critically about World Wide Web Resources.* <http://www.library.ucla.edu/libraries/college/instruct/web/critical.htm>, (last updated 1 Oct 1998, accessed 10 Oct 1998).

10. Greenleaf, Graham and Geoffrey King (1996). *User Guide to AustLII's Legal Links.* <http://www.*AustLII*.edu.au/help/links.html#/Australia_index>, (Version — 10 Oct 1996, accessed 10 Oct 1998).

11. Information Quality WWW Virtual Library: *The Internet Guide to Construction of Quality Online Resources,* ed T. Matthew Ciolek. <http://www.ciolek.com/WWWVL-InfoQuality.html>, (est.: 15 March 1996, last updated: 15 Nov 1998, accessed 16 Nov 1998).

12. Kahle, Brewster (1997). 'Preserving the Internet'. *Scientific American,* March 1997. <http://www.sciam.com/0397issue/0397kahle.html>, (accessed 7 Feb 1998).

13. Lahita, Robert (1996). *Symptoms of Lupus.*
    <http://www.hamline.edu/lupus/articles/symptoms_of
    _lupus.html>, (updated 30 July 1996, accessed 10 Oct 1998).

14. Lyman, Peter and Brewster Kahle (1998). 'Archiving digital
    cultural artifacts: organizing an agenda for action'. *D-Lib
    Magazine,* July/August 1998.
    <http://www.dlib.org/dlib/july98/07lyman.html>,
    (accessed 14 Sept 1998).

15. McNally, Paul (1997). *Multimedia Information Resources.* South
    Melbourne: Macmillan Education Australia, 1997.

16. Mintzer, Fred, et al. (1997). 'Safeguarding digital library
    contents and users'. *D-Lib Magazine,* December 1997.
    <http://www.dlib.org/dlib/december97/ibm/12lotspiech.html
    >, (accessed 15 Feb 1998).

17. Nelson, Ted (1965). 'A file structure for the complex, the changing
    and the indeterminate'. *ACM 20th National Conference,* 1965.

18. Nelson, Ted (1980). 'Replacing the printed word: a complete
    literary system'. *Information Processing '80,* 1980.

19. Network Working Group (1994). *Request for Comments: 1738:
    Uniform Resource Locators (URL).*
    <ftp://ftp.demon.co.uk/pub/doc/rfc/rfc1738.txt>, (Dated
    Dec 1994, accessed 14 Jan 1997).

20. Oakerson, Ann (1996). 'Who owns digital works?' *Scientific
    American,* 275(1) (July 1996): 80–84.

21. Pfaffenberger, Bryan (1996). *Web Search Strategies.* New York: MIS:Press, 1996. Chapter 4 'Finding something relevant'. <http://www.mispress.com/websearch/websch4.html>, (accessed 14 Jan 1997).

22. Quinion, Michael B. (1996). *Citing Online Sources: Advice on Online Citations Formats.* <http://clever.net/quinion/words/articles/citation.htm>, (updated 11 Feb 1998, accessed 10 Oct 1998).

23. Scholz-Crane, Ann (1996). *Evaluating World Wide Web information.* <http://www.lib.purdue.edu:80/research/classes/gs175/ 2gs175/evaluation.html>, (last update: 30 Sept 1996, accessed 10 Oct 1996).

24. Smith, Alastair (1997). 'Testing the surf: criteria for evaluation of Internet Information Resources'. *The Public-Access Computer Systems Review* 8, no. 3, 1997. <http://info.lib.uh.edu/pr/v8/n3/smit8n3.html>, (accessed 12 Oct 1998).

25. Terrass, Richard (1997). *Evaluating Internet resources.* <http://users.aol.com:80/ricter/private/home/valid.html>, (last updated 10 May 1997, accessed 10 Oct 1998).

26. Torres, Deborah A. (1995). *Possible Technology-based Solutions for the Display and Distribution of Copyrighted Electronic Images.* <http://www.sims.berkeley.edu/impact/f95/Papers- projects/Papers/torres.html>, (dated 22 Oct 1995, accessed 10 Oct 1998).

27. University of California, Berkeley, Library (1998). *Searching the World Wide Web: Strategies, Analyzing Your Topic, Choosing Search Tools.*
<http://www.lib.berkeley.edu/TeachingLib/Guides/Internet/Strategies.html>, (last updated 26 Oct 1998, accessed 15 Nov 1998).

28. University of Sydney Library (1998). *Searching the Internet: References.*
<http://www.library.usyd.edu.au/Index/searchbib.html>, (last modified 6 Aug 1998, accessed 10 Oct 1998).

29. Webster, Kathleen and K. Paul (1996). 'Beyond surfing: tools and techniques for searching the Web'. *Information Technology,* Jan 1996.
<http://magi.com/~mmelick/it96jan.htm>, (accessed 13 Mar 1996).

30. *WIPO Copyright Treaty, Adopted by the Diplomatic Conference on December 20, 1996.*
<http://ananse.irv.uit.no/trade_law/doc/WIPO.Copyright.Treaty.1996.toc.html>, (dated 1 Mar 1997 accessed 10 Oct 1998).

Index